Chicken

MARKS &
SPENCER

Marks and Spencer p.l.c.
Baker Street, London W1U 8EP
www.marksandspencer.com

Produced by The Bridgewater Book Company Ltd.

Photography: St John Asprey
Home Economist: Jaqueline Bellefontaine

ISBN: 1-84273-213-7

Printed in China

NOTE
Tablespoons are assumed to be 15 ml.
Unless otherwise stated, milk is assumed
to be full-fat, eggs are medium and pepper
is freshly ground black pepper.

contents

introduction

One of the easiest and least disruptive ways to reduce your fat intake is to change the way you cook. Trying new recipes, even with familiar ingredients, is fun and will result in the pleasure of eating delicious meals that are also healthier.

Chicken has become justly popular around the world and plays an important part in the modern diet, being reasonably priced and nutritionally sound. A versatile meat, it lends itself to an enormous range of cooking methods and cuisines. Its unassertive flavour means that it is equally suited to cooking with both sweet

and savoury flavours. Because it has a low fat content, especially without the skin, it is an ideal meat for low cholesterol and calorie-controlled diets. As well as being an excellent source of protein, chicken contains valuable minerals, such as potassium and phosphorus, and some of the B vitamins.

Roasting

Remove any fat from the body cavity. Rinse the bird inside and out with water, then pat dry with kitchen paper. Season the cavity generously with salt and pepper and add stuffing, herbs or lemon if wished. Spread the breast of the chicken with softened butter or oil. Set on a rack in a roasting tin or shallow baking dish. Roast the bird, basting two or three times with the pan juices during roasting. If the chicken is browning too quickly, cover it with foil. Use a meat thermometer or insert a skewer into the thickest part of the thigh to see if the meat is done. If the chicken is cooked, the juices will run clear with no trace of pink. Put the bird on a carving board and leave to rest for 15 minutes before serving. Make a sauce or otherwise a gravy from the juices left in the roasting tin.

Grilling

The intense heat of the grill quickly seals the succulent flesh beneath a crisp, golden exterior. Place the chicken 10–15 cm/4–6 inches away from a moderate heat source. If the chicken seems to be browning too quickly, reduce the heat slightly. If the chicken is grilled at too high a temperature too near to the heat, the outside will burn before the inside is cooked. If it is cooked for too long under a low heat, it will dry out. Divide the chicken into joints to ensure even cooking. Breast meat, if cooked in one piece, can be rather dry, so it is best to cut it into chunks for kebabs. Wings are best for speedy grilling.

Frying

Suitable for small thighs, drumsticks and joints. Dry the chicken pieces with kitchen paper so that they brown properly and to prevent spitting during cooking. The chicken can be coated in seasoned flour, egg and breadcrumbs or a batter. Heat oil or a mixture of oil and butter in a deep frying pan. When the oil is very hot, add the chicken pieces, skin-side down. Fry until deep golden brown all over, turning the pieces frequently during cooking. Drain well on kitchen paper before serving.

Sautéing

Ideal for small pieces or small birds. Heat a little oil or a mixture of oil and butter in a heavy frying pan. Add the chicken and fry over a moderate heat until golden brown, turning frequently. Add stock or other liquid, bring to the boil, then cover and reduce the heat. Cook gently until the chicken is cooked through.

Stir-Frying

Good when skinless, boneless chicken is cut into small pieces of equal size to ensure that the meat cooks evenly and stays succulent. Preheat a wok or frying pan before adding a small amount of oil. When the oil starts to smoke, add the chicken and stir-fry with your chosen flavourings for 3–4 minutes until cooked through. Other ingredients can be cooked at the same time, or the chicken can be cooked by itself, then removed from the pan while you stir-fry the remaining ingredients. Return the chicken to the pan once the other ingredients are cooked.

Casseroling

A good method for cooking joints from larger, more mature chickens, although smaller chickens can be cooked whole. The slow cooking produces tender meat with a good flavour. Brown the chicken in butter or oil or a mixture of both. Add some stock, wine or a mixture of both with seasonings and herbs, cover and cook on top of the stove or in the oven until the chicken is tender. Add a selection of lightly sautéed vegetables about halfway through the cooking time.

Braising

A method which requires little or no liquid. The chicken pieces or a small whole chicken and vegetables are cooked together slowly in a low oven. Heat some oil in an ovenproof, flameproof casserole and gently fry the chicken until golden. Remove the chicken and fry a selection of vegetables until they are almost tender. Replace the chicken, cover tightly and cook very gently on the top of the stove or in a low oven until the chicken and vegetables are tender.

Poaching

A gentle cooking method that produces tender chicken and a stock that can be used to make a sauce to serve with the chicken. Put a whole chicken, a bouquet garni, a leek, a carrot and an onion in a large flameproof casserole. Cover with water, season and bring to the boil. Simmer for 1½–2 hours until the chicken is tender. Lift out the chicken, discard the bouquet garni and use the stock to make a sauce. Blend the vegetables to thicken the stock and serve with the chicken.

Food Safety & Tips

Chicken can become contaminated by salmonella bacteria, which can cause severe food poisoning. When storing, handling and preparing poultry, certain precautions must be observed to prevent the possibility of food poisoning.

• Check the sell-by date and best before date. After buying, take the chicken home quickly, preferably in a freezer bag or cool box.

• Return frozen birds to the freezer immediately.

• If storing in the refrigerator, remove the wrappings and store any giblets separately. Place the chicken in a shallow dish to catch drips. Cover loosely with foil and store on the bottom shelf of the refrigerator for no more than two or three days, depending on the best before date. Avoid any contact between raw chicken and cooked food during storage and preparation. Wash your hands thoroughly after handling raw chicken.

• Prepare raw chicken on a chopping board that can be easily cleaned and bleached, such as a non-porous, plastic board.

• Frozen birds should be defrosted before cooking. If time permits, defrost for about 36 hours in the refrigerator, or thaw for about 12 hours in a cool place. Bacteria breed in warm food at room temperature and when chicken is thawing. Cooking at high temperatures kills bacteria. There should be no ice crystals and the flesh should feel soft and flexible. Cook the chicken as soon as possible after thawing.

• Make sure that chicken is cooked. Test if the chicken is done using a meat thermometer – the thigh should reach at least 79°C/175°F when cooked. Otherwise, pierce the thickest part of a thigh with a skewer – the juices should run clear, not pink or red. Never partially cook chicken with the intention of completing cooking later.

Chicken soup has a long tradition of being comforting and good for us and some cultures even think of it as a cure for all ills. It is certainly satisfying, full of flavour and easy to digest. For the best results, use a good homemade chicken stock, although when time is at

a premium, a good quality stock cube can be used instead. Every cuisine in the world has its own favourite version of chicken soup and in this section you'll find a selection of recipes from as far afield as Italy, Scotland and China.

As chicken is so versatile and quick to cook, it is perfect for innovative and appetising snacks. Its unassertive flavour means that it can be enlivened by exotic fruits and spices and oriental ingredients, such as mirin, sesame oil and fresh ginger root. There are fritters, salads and drumsticks that are stuffed and baked, or served with delicious fruity salsas. Because chicken pieces travel well and are easy to eat, many of the recipes are ideal to take on picnics or to pack into a lunch box.

soups, starters & salads

scottish chicken & barley broth

This soup is made with traditional Scottish ingredients. It should be left for at least two days before being reheated, then served with oatmeal cakes or bread.

Serves 4

60 g/2 oz pre-soaked dried peas

900 g/2 lb diced chicken,
    fat removed

1.2 litres/2 pints chicken stock

600 ml/1 pint water

60 g/2 oz barley, washed

1 large carrot, peeled and diced

1 small turnip, peeled and diced

1 large leek, thinly sliced

1 red onion, chopped finely

salt and white pepper

1 Put the peas and chicken into a pan, add the stock and water and bring slowly to the boil.

2 Skim the stock as it boils using a slotted spoon.

3 When all the scum is removed, add the washed barley and salt and simmer for 35 minutes.

4 Add the remaining ingredients and simmer for 2 hours.

5 Skim the surface of the soup again and allow the broth to stand for at least 24 hours. Reheat, adjust the seasoning and serve.

2

3

4

variation

This soup is just as delicious made with beef or lamb. Substitute 225 g/8 oz lean sirloin beef or lean lamb fillet for the chicken. Trim any fat from the meat and cut into thin strips before using.

cook's tip

Use either whole grain barley or pearl barley. Only the outer husk is removed from whole grain barley and when cooked it has a nutty flavour and a chewy texture.

chicken & sherry consommé

This is a very flavoursome soup, especially if you make it from real chicken stock. Egg shells are used to give a crystal clear appearance.

Serves 8-10

1.75 litres/3 pints chicken stock

150 ml/¼ pint medium sherry

4 egg whites plus egg shells

125 g/4 oz cooked chicken, sliced thinly

salt and pepper

garnish (see Cook's Tip)

2

1 Place the chicken stock and sherry in a large saucepan and heat gently for 5 minutes.

2 Add the egg whites and the egg shells to the chicken stock and whisk until the mixture begins to boil.

3

3 Remove the pan from the heat and allow the mixture to subside for 10 minutes. Repeat this process three times. This allows the egg white to trap the sediments in the chicken stock to clarify the soup. Let the consommé cool for 5 minutes.

4 Carefully place a piece of fine muslin over a clean saucepan. Ladle the soup over the muslin and strain into the saucepan.

4

5 Repeat this process twice, then gently reheat the consommé. Season with salt and pepper to taste then add the cooked chicken slices. Pour the soup into a warm serving dish or individual bowls.

6 Garnish the consommé with any of the suggestions listed in the Cook's Tip, far left.

cook's tip

Consommé is usually garnished with freshly cooked pasta shapes, noodles, rice or lightly cooked vegetables. Alternatively, you could garnish it with omelette strips, drained first on paper towels.

irish chicken soup

The potato has been part of the Irish diet for centuries. This recipe is originally from the north of Ireland, in the beautiful area of Moira, County Down.

Serves 4

3 smoked, streaky,
   rindless bacon slices, chopped

500 g/1 lb 2 oz boneless chicken, chopped

25 g/1 oz butter

3 medium potatoes, chopped

3 medium onions, chopped

600 ml/1 pint giblet or
   chicken stock

600 ml/1 pint milk

salt and pepper

150 ml/¼ pint double cream

2 tbsp chopped fresh parsley

soda bread, to serve

variation

For a more filling, main course soup, you can add any number of different vegetables, for example leeks, celeriac or sweetcorn.

1 Gently dry fry the bacon and chicken in a large saucepan for 10 minutes.

2 Add the butter, potatoes and onions and cook for 15 minutes, stirring all the time.

1

2

3 Add the stock and milk, then bring the soup to the boil and simmer for 45 minutes. Season with salt and pepper to taste.

4 Blend in the cream and simmer for 5 minutes. Stir in the chopped fresh parsley, then transfer the soup to a warm tureen or individual bowls and serve with Irish soda bread.

4

cook's tip

Soda bread is not made with yeast as bread usually is. Instead it is made with bicarbonate of soda as the raising agent. It can be made with plain or wholemeal flour.

spicy mulligatawny soup

This spicy soup was brought to the west by army and service personnel returning from India. It's perfect for a cold day

Serves 4

60 g/2 oz butter

1 onion, sliced

1 garlic clove, crushed

500 g/1 lb 2 oz chicken, diced

60 g/2 oz smoked, rindless bacon, diced

1 small turnip, diced

2 carrots, diced

1 small cooking apple, diced

2 tbsp mild curry powder

1 tbsp curry paste

1 tbsp tomato purée

1 tbsp plain flour

1.2 litres/2 pints chicken stock

salt and pepper

150 ml/¼ pint double cream

1 tsp chopped fresh coriander, to garnish

1 Melt the butter in a large saucepan and cook the onion, garlic, chicken and bacon for 5 minutes.

2 Add the turnip, carrots and apple and cook for a further two minutes.

3 Blend in the curry powder, curry paste and tomato purée and sprinkle over the plain flour.

4 Add the chicken stock and bring to the boil, cover and simmer over a gentle heat for about 1 hour.

5 Liquidise the soup. Reheat, season well with salt and pepper to taste and gradually blend in the double cream. Garnish the soup with chopped fresh coriander and serve over small bowls of boiled or fried rice.

3

4

cook's tip

This soup may be frozen for up to 1 month; if stored for any longer, the spices may cause it to taste musty.

2

herbed chicken & pasta soup

This light, clear soup has a delicate flavour of asparagus and herbs. Use a good quality stock for best results.

Serves 4

225 g/8 oz fresh asparagus

850 ml/1½ pints fresh
    chicken stock

150 ml/5 fl oz dry white wine

1 sprig each fresh parsley, dill and
    tarragon

1 garlic clove

60 g/2 oz vermicelli rice noodles

350 g/12 oz lean cooked chicken,
    finely shredded

salt and white pepper

1 small leek, shredded, to garnish

1

3

4

1 Wash the asparagus and trim away
the woody ends. Cut each spear
into pieces 4 cm/1½ inches long.

2 Pour the stock and wine into a large
saucepan and bring to the boil.

3 Wash the herbs and tie them
with clean string. Peel the garlic
clove and add, with the herbs, to the
saucepan together with the asparagus
and noodles. Cover and simmer
for 5 minutes.

4 Stir in the chicken and plenty of
seasoning. Simmer gently for a
further 3-4 minutes until heated through.

5 Trim the leek, slice it down the
centre and wash under running
water to remove any dirt. Shake dry
and shred finely.

6 Remove the herbs and garlic from
the pan and discard. Ladle the soup
into warm bowls, sprinkle with shredded
leek and serve at once.

variation

You can use any of your
favourite herbs in this
recipe, but choose those
with a subtle flavour so
that they do not overpower
the asparagus. Small, tender
asparagus spears give the
best results and flavour.

cook's tip

Rice noodles contain no fat
and are an ideal substitute
for egg noodles.

chicken & prune soup

This satisfying soup can be served as a main course. You can add rice and peppers to make it even more hearty, as well as colourful.

Serves 6

350 g/12 oz boneless chicken

350 g/12 oz leeks

30 g/1 oz butter

1.2 litres/2 pints chicken stock

1 bouquet garni sachet

salt and white pepper

8 stoned prunes, halved

cooked rice and diced peppers (optional)

cook's tip

If you have time, make the chicken stock yourself. Alternatively, you can buy good fresh stock from supermarkets.

1 Using a sharp knife, cut the chicken and leeks into 2.5 cm/1 inch pieces.

2 Melt the butter in a large saucepan, add the chicken and leeks and fry for 8 minutes, stirring occasionally.

3 Add the chicken stock and bouquet garni sachet to the mixture in the pan, and season with salt and pepper to taste.

5

2

4 Bring the soup to the boil and simmer over a gentle heat for 45 minutes.

5 Add the stoned prunes with some cooked rice and diced peppers (if using), and simmer for 20 minutes. Remove the bouquet garni sachet and discard. Pour the soup into a warm tureen or individual bowls and serve.

3

variation

Instead of the bouquet garni sachet, you can use a bunch of fresh, mixed herbs, tied together with string. Choose herbs such as parsley, thyme and rosemary.

chicken & tarragon soup

Tarragon adds a delicate aniseed flavour to this tasty soup. If you can't find tarragon, use parsley for a fresh taste.

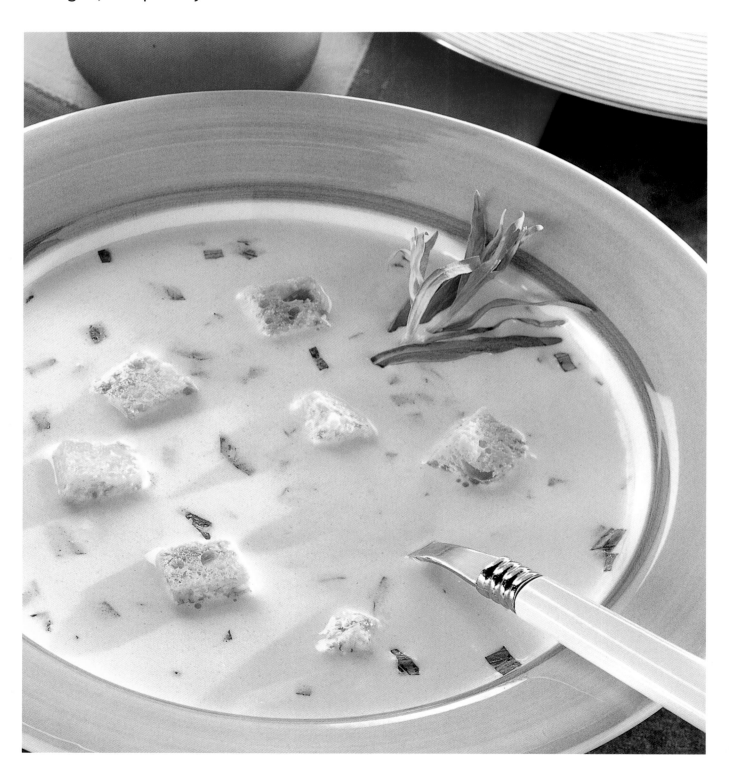

Serves 4

60 g/2 oz unsalted butter

1 large onion, peeled and chopped

300 g/10½ oz cooked chicken,
    shredded finely

600 ml/1 pint chicken stock

salt and pepper

1 tbsp chopped fresh tarragon

150 ml/¼ pint double cream

fresh tarragon leaves, to garnish

deep-fried croûtons, to serve

1

2

5

1 Melt the butter in a large saucepan and fry the onion for 3 minutes.

2 Add the chicken to the pan with 300 ml/½ pint of the chicken stock.

3 Bring to the boil and simmer for 20 minutes. Allow to cool, then liquidise the soup.

4 Add the remainder of the stock and season with salt and pepper.

5 Add the chopped tarragon, pour the soup into a tureen or individual serving bowls and add a swirl of cream.

6 Garnish the soup with fresh tarragon and serve with deep-fried croûtons.

cook's tip

To make garlic croûtons, crush 3-4 garlic cloves in a pestle and mortar and add to the oil before frying.

variation

If you can't find fresh tarragon, freeze-dried tarragon makes a good substitute. Single cream can be used instead of double cream.

fresh tomato & chicken soup

This soup is very good made wih fresh tomatoes, but if you prefer, you can use canned tomatoes, although the flavour isn't as good.

Serves 2

60 g/2 oz unsalted butter

1 large onion, chopped

500 g/1 lb 2 oz chicken,
    shredded very finely

600 ml/1 pint chicken stock

6 medium tomatoes, chopped finely

pinch of bicarbonate of soda

salt and pepper

1 tbsp caster sugar

150 ml/1¼ pint double cream

fresh basil leaves, to garnish

croûtons, to serve

1 Melt the butter in a large saucepan and fry the onion and shredded chicken for 5 minutes.

2 Add 300 ml/½ pint chicken stock to the pan, with the tomatoes and bicarbonate of soda.

5

2

3 Bring the soup to the boil and simmer for 20 minutes.

4 Allow the soup to cool, then blend in a food processor.

5 Add the remaining chicken stock, season with salt and pepper, then add the sugar. Pour the soup into a tureen and add a swirl of double cream. Garnish with fresh basil leaves and serve the soup with croûtons.

cook's tip

For a healthier version of this soup, use single cream instead of the double cream and omit the sugar.

4

variation

For an Italian-style soup, add 1 tbsp chopped fresh basil with the stock in step 2. Alternatively, add ½ tsp curry powder or chilli powder to make a spicier version of this soup.

chicken & turnip soup with coriander balls

Use the strained vegetables and chicken to make little patties. Simply mash with a little butter, shape them into round cakes and fry until golden brown.

Serves 6-8

900 g/2 lb chicken meat, sliced

60 g/2 oz plain flour

125 g/4½ oz butter

3 tbsp sunflower oil

1 large carrot, chopped

1 stick celery, chopped

1 onion, chopped

1 small turnip, chopped

120 ml/4 fl oz sherry

1 tsp thyme

1 bay leaf

salt and pepper

1.75 litres/3 pints chicken stock

crusty bread, to serve

DUMPLINGS

60 g/2 oz self-raising flour

60 g/2 oz fresh breadcrumbs

2 tbsp shredded suet

2 tbsp chopped fresh coriander

2 tbsp finely grated lemon rind

salt and pepper

1 egg

1

5
7

1 Coat the chicken pieces with the flour and season.

2 Melt the butter in a saucepan and fry the chicken pieces until they are lightly browned.

3 Add the oil to the pan and brown the vegetables. Add the sherry and the remaining ingredients except the stock.

4 Cook for 10 minutes, then add the stock. Simmer for 3 hours, then strain into a clean saucepan and allow to cool.

5 To make the dumplings, mix together all the dry ingredients in a large clean bowl. Add the egg and blend in thoroughly then add enough milk to make a moist dough.

6 Shape into small balls and roll them in a little flour.

7 Cook the dumplings in boiling salted water for 10 minutes.

8 Remove them carefully with a slotted spoon and add them to the soup. Cook for a further 12 minutes, then serve with crusty bread.

lemon chicken soup

This refreshing soup with its refreshing lemon flavour is perfect on summer days.

Serves 4

60 g/2 oz butter

8 shallots, sliced thinly

2 medium carrots, sliced thinly

2 stalks celery, sliced thinly

250 g/9 oz skinless chicken breast meat,
   chopped finely

3 lemons

1.2 litres/2 pints chicken stock

150 ml/¼ pint double cream

salt and pepper

sprigs of parsley and lemon slices,
   to garnish

variation

For an alternative citrus flavour, use 4 oranges in place of the lemons. The recipe can also be adapted to make duck and orange soup.

1

2

1 Melt the butter in a large saucepan, add the vegetables and chicken and cook gently for 8 minutes.

2 Thinly pare the lemons and blanch the lemon rind in boiling water for 3 minutes.

3 Squeeze the juice from the lemons.

4 Add the lemon rind and freshly squeezed lemon juice to the pan with the chicken stock.

4

5 Bring slowly to the boil and simmer for about 50 minutes. Leave the soup to cool then transfer to a food processor and blend until smooth. Return the soup to the saucepan, reheat, season with salt and pepper to taste and add the double cream. Do not boil at this stage or the soup will curdle.

6 Transfer the soup to a tureen or warm individual bowls. Serve, garnished with parsley and lemon slices.

chicken & pasta soup with guinea fowl

Guinea fowl has a similar texture to chicken, and although it has a milder flavour than other game, it has a slightly gamier flavour than chicken.

Serves 6

500 g/1 lb 2 oz skinless chicken, chopped

500 g/1 lb 2 oz skinless guinea fowl meat

600 ml/1 pint chicken stock

1 small onion

6 peppercorns

1 tsp cloves

pinch of mace

150 ml/¼ pint double cream

15 g/½ oz butter

2 tsp plain flour

125 g/4½ oz quick-cook spaghetti, broken into short lengths and cooked

2 tbsp chopped fresh parsley, to garnish

variation

Instead of spaghetti, use small pasta shapes such as ziti or macaroni.

4

5

6

1 Put the chicken and guinea fowl meat into a large saucepan with the chicken stock.

2 Bring to the boil and add the onion, peppercorns, cloves and mace. Simmer gently for about 2 hours until the stock is reduced by one-third.

3 Strain the soup, skim off any fat and remove any bones from the chicken and guinea fowl.

4 Return the soup and meat to a clean saucepan. Add the double cream and bring to the boil slowly.

5 To make a roux, melt the butter and stir in the flour until it has a paste-like consistency. Add to the soup, stirring until slightly thickened.

6 Just before serving, add the cooked quick-cook spaghetti.

7 Transfer the soup to individual serving bowls, garnish with parsley and serve.

chinese wonton soup

This Chinese-style soup is delicious as a starter to an oriental meal or as a light meal.

Serves 4-6

FILLING

350 g/12 oz minced chicken

1 tbsp soy sauce

1 tsp grated, fresh ginger root

1 garlic clove, crushed

2 tsp sherry

2 spring onions, chopped

1 tsp sesame oil

1 egg white

½ tsp cornflour

½ tsp sugar

about 35 wonton wrappers

SOUP

1.5 litres/2¾ pints chicken stock

1 tbsp light soy sauce

1 spring onion, shredded

1 small carrot, cut into very thin slices

3

4

6

1 Combine all the ingredients for the filling and mix well.

2 Place a small spoonful of the filling in the centre of each wonton wrapper.

3 Dampen the edges and gather up the wonton wrapper to form a pouch enclosing the filling.

4 Cook the filled wontons in boiling water for 1 minute or until they float to the top. Remove with a slotted spoon.

5 Bring the chicken stock to the boil.

6 Add the soy sauce, spring onion, carrot and wontons to the soup. Simmer gently for 2 minutes then serve.

variation

Substitute the chicken for minced pork.

cook's tip

Look for wonton wrappers in Chinese or oriental supermarkets. Fresh wrappers can be found in the chilled compartment and they can be frozen if you wish. Wrap in clingfilm before freezing.

orange chicken & carrot soup

For a tangy flavour, lemons can be used instead of oranges and the recipe can be adapted to make duck and orange soup.

2

Serves 4

60 g/2 oz butter

8 shallots, sliced thinly

2 medium carrots, sliced thinly

2 sticks celery, sliced thinly

250 g/8 oz skinless chicken breast,
    chopped finely

3 oranges

1.2 litres/2 pints chicken stock

salt and white pepper

150 ml/¼ pint double cream

sprig of parsley and 3 orange slices,
    to garnish

soda bread, to serve

3

5

variation

Use 2 small lemons in place
of the oranges. Look for
organic or unwaxed lemons
when using rind.

1 Melt the butter in a large saucepan, add the shallots, carrot, celery and chicken meat and cook gently for 8 minutes, stirring occasionally.

2 Using a potato peeler or sharp knife, thinly pare the oranges and blanch the rind in boiling water for about 3 minutes.

3 Squeeze the juice from the oranges. Add the orange rind and orange juice to the pan together with the chicken stock.

4 Bring slowly to the boil and simmer for 50 minutes. Cool the soup then liquidise in a blender or food processor until smooth.

5 Return the soup to the saucepan, reheat, season to taste and add the cream. Do not boil at this stage or the soup will curdle.

6 Transfer the soup to a serving dish or individual bowls. Garnish with a sprig of parsley and orange slices, and serve with soda bread.

chicken & bean soup

This hearty and nourishing soup is an ideal starter for a family supper.

Serves 4

25 g/1 oz butter

3 spring onions, chopped

2 garlic cloves, crushed

1 fresh marjoram sprig,
    finely chopped

350 g/12 oz boned chicken breasts, diced

1.2 litres/2 pints chicken stock

350 g/12 oz can chickpeas, drained

1 bouquet garni

salt and white pepper

1 red pepper, diced

1 green pepper, diced

115 g/4 oz small dried pasta shapes,
    such as elbow macaroni

croûtons, to serve

cook's tip

If you prefer, you can use dried chickpeas. Cover with cold water and set aside to soak for 5-8 hours. Drain and add the beans to the soup, according to the recipe, and allow an additional 30 minutes-1 hour cooking time.

1

2

1 Melt the butter in a large saucepan. Add the spring onions, garlic, marjoram and the diced chicken and cook, stirring frequently, over a medium heat for 5 minutes.

2 Add the chicken stock, chickpeas and bouquet garni to the pan and season to taste with salt and white pepper.

4

3 Bring the soup to the boil, lower the heat and then simmer gently for about 2 hours.

4 Add the diced peppers and pasta to the pan, then simmer for a further 20 minutes.

5 Transfer the soup to a warm tureen. To serve, ladle the soup into individual serving bowls and garnish with the croûtons.

creamy chicken & pasta soup

This delicately flavoured summer soup is surprisingly easy to make.

Serves 4

60 g/2 oz butter

8 shallots, thinly sliced

2 carrots, thinly sliced

2 celery sticks, thinly sliced

225 g/8 oz boned chicken breasts,
    finely chopped

3 lemons

1.2 litres/2 pints chicken stock

225 g/8 oz dried spaghetti, broken into
    small pieces

salt and white pepper

150 ml/¼ pint double cream

fresh parsley sprig and 3 lemon slices,
    halved, to garnish

1 Melt the butter in a large saucepan. Add the shallots, carrots, celery and chicken and cook over a low heat, stirring occasionally, for 8 minutes.

2 Thinly pare the lemons and blanch the lemon rind in boiling water for 3 minutes. Squeeze the juice from the lemons.

3 Add the lemon rind and juice to the pan, together with the chicken stock. Bring slowly to the boil over a low heat and simmer for 40 minutes.

4 Add the spaghetti to the pan and cook for 15 minutes. Season to taste with salt and white pepper and add the cream. Heat through, but do not allow the soup to boil or it will curdle.

5 Pour the soup into a tureen or individual bowls, garnish with the parsley and half slices of lemon and serve immediately.

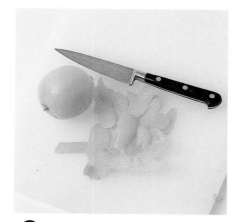

2

cook's tip

You can prepare this soup up to the end of step 3 in advance, so that all you need do before serving is heat it through before adding the pasta and the finishing touches.

1

4

chicken, onion & bacon soup

A hearty soup that is so simple to make yet packed with flavour.
You can use either whole green peas or green or yellow split peas.

Serves 4-6

3 smoked, streaky, rindless bacon
   slices, chopped

900 g/2 lb chicken, chopped

1 large onion, chopped

15 g/½ oz butter

500 g/1 lb 2 oz ready-soaked peas

2.4 litres/4 pints chicken stock

salt and pepper

150 ml/¼ pint double cream

2 tbsp chopped fresh parsley

cheesy croûtes, to garnish (see Cook's Tip)

1 Put the bacon, chicken and onion into a large saucepan with a little butter and cook over a gentle heat for 8 minutes.

2 Add the peas and the stock to the pan, bring to the boil, season lightly with salt and pepper, cover and simmer for 2 hours.

3

3 Blend the double cream into the soup, sprinkle with parsley and top with cheesy croûtes (see Cook's Tip, left).

1

2

cook's tip

Croûtes are slices of French bread that are fried or baked, then sprinkled with grated cheese and lightly toasted.

variation

Use 100 g/3½ oz chopped ham instead of the bacon, if you prefer.

cook's tip

If using dried peas, soak them for several hours or overnight in a large bowl of cold water. Alternatively, bring them to the boil in a pan of cold water. Remove from the heat and leave to cool in the water. Drain and rinse the beans before adding them to the soup.

thai-spiced chicken soup

Quick to make, this hot and spicy soup is hearty and warming. If you like your food really fiery, add a chopped dried or fresh chilli with its seeds.

Serves 4

1 sheet of dried egg noodles from
a 250 g/9 oz pack

1 tbsp oil

4 skinless, boneless chicken thighs, diced

1 bunch spring onions, sliced

2 garlic cloves, chopped

2 cm/¾ inch piece fresh ginger root,
finely chopped

850 ml/1½ pints chicken stock

200 ml/7 fl oz coconut milk

3 tsp red Thai curry paste

3 tbsp peanut butter

2 tbsp light soy sauce

salt and pepper

1 small red pepper, chopped

60 g/2 oz frozen peas

1

2

3

1 Put the noodles in a shallow dish and soak in boiling water following the instructions on the packet.

2 Heat the oil in a large saucepan or wok, add the chicken, and fry for 5 minutes, stirring until lightly browned. Add the white part of the spring onions, the garlic and ginger and fry for 2 minutes, stirring. Add the stock, coconut milk, curry paste, peanut butter and soy sauce. Season with salt and pepper to taste. Bring to the boil, stirring, then simmer for 8 minutes,

stirring occasionally. Add the red pepper, peas and green spring onion tops and cook for 2 minutes.

3 Add the drained noodles and heat through. Spoon into individual bowls and serve with a spoon and fork.

variation

Green Thai curry paste can be used instead of red curry paste for a less fiery flavour.

chicken vermicelli soup

This heart-warming soup is both quick and easy to make.

Serves 4

450 g/1 lb boned chicken breasts,
   cut into strips

1.2 litres/2 pints chicken stock

150 ml/¼ pint double cream

salt and pepper

100 g/3½ oz dried vermicelli

1 tbsp cornflour

3 tbsp milk

175 g/6 oz sweetcorn kernels

cook's tip

If you are short of time, buy ready-cooked chicken, remove any skin and cut it into slices.

variation

For crab and sweetcorn soup, substitute 450 g/1 lb cooked crabmeat for the chicken breasts. Flake the crabmeat well before adding it to the saucepan and reduce the cooking time by 10 minutes. For a Chinese-style soup, substitute egg noodles for the vermicelli and use canned, creamed sweetcorn.

1

4

4

1 Put the chicken, stock and cream into a large saucepan and bring to the boil over a low heat. Reduce the heat slightly and simmer for about 20 minutes. Season the soup with salt and black pepper to taste.

2 Meanwhile, cook the vermicelli in lightly salted boiling water for 10–12 minutes, until just tender. Drain the pasta and keep warm.

3 In a small bowl, mix together the cornflour and milk to make a smooth paste. Stir the cornflour into the soup until thickened.

4 Add the sweetcorn and vermicelli to the pan and heat through.

5 Transfer the soup to a warm tureen or individual soup bowls and serve immediately.

chicken & mixed vegetable broth

This satisfying soup makes a good lunch or supper dish and you can use any vegetables that you have at hand. Children will love the tiny pasta shapes.

Serves 6

350 g/12 oz boneless
   chicken breasts

2 tbsp sunflower oil

1 medium onion, diced

250 g/9 oz carrots, diced

250 g/9 oz cauliflower florets

850 ml/1½ pints chicken stock

2 tsp dried mixed herbs

125 g/4½ oz small pasta shapes

salt and pepper

Parmesan cheese (optional)

Crusty bread, to serve

1

3

2

1 Using a sharp knife, finely dice the chicken, discarding any skin.

2 Heat the oil in a large saucepan and quickly sauté the chicken and vegetables until they are lightly coloured.

3 Stir in the stock and herbs. Bring to the boil and add the pasta shapes. Return to the boil, cover and simmer for 10 minutes, stirring occasionally to prevent the pasta shapes sticking together.

4 Season with salt and pepper to taste and sprinkle with Parmesan cheese, if using. Serve with fresh crusty bread.

cook's tip

You can use any small pasta shapes for this soup — try conchigliette or ditalini or even spaghetti broken up into small pieces. To make a fun soup for children you could add animal-shaped or alphabet pasta.

variation

Broccoli florets can be used to replace the cauliflower florets. Substitute 2 tbsp chopped fresh mixed herbs for the dried mixed herbs.

mixed cheese & parsley drumsticks

Ideal for informal parties, these tasty chicken drumsticks can be prepared for cooking a day in advance. Instead of baking the chicken drumsticks, you could cook them on the barbecue instead.

Serves 6

15 g/½ oz butter

1 garlic clove, crushed

3 tbsp chopped fresh parsley

125 g/4½ oz ricotta cheese

4 tbsp grated Parmesan cheese

3 tbsp fresh breadcrumbs

salt and pepper

12 chicken drumsticks

lemon slices, to garnish

mixed salad leaves, to serve

variation

Any strongly flavoured cheese can be used instead of the Parmesan. Try a mature Cheddar or use another Italian cheese, such as pecorino

cook's tip

Freshly grated Parmesan has more 'bite' than ready-packed grated Parmesan from supermarkets. Grate only as much as you need and wrap the rest up in foil — it will then keep for several months in the refrigerator.

1 Melt the butter in a pan. Add the garlic and fry gently, stirring, for 1 minute without browning.

2 Remove the pan from the heat and stir in the parsley, the cheeses, breadcrumbs and salt and pepper to taste.

3 Carefully loosen the skin around the chicken drumsticks.

4 Using a teaspoon, push about 1 tablespoon of the stuffing under the skin of each drumstick. Arrange the drumsticks in a large baking tin.

5 Bake in a preheated oven, 190°C/375°F/Gas Mark 5, for about 45 minutes. Garnish with lemon slices and serve hot or cold, with mixed salad leaves.

3

4

2

cheese & chicken toasts

A tasty dish that can be served alone as a snack or to accompany a light, clear soup.

1

Serves 4

250 g/9 oz grated Wensleydale cheese

250 g/9 oz shredded, cooked chicken

25g/1 oz butter

1 tbsp Worcestershire sauce

1 tsp dry English mustard

2 tsp plain flour

4 tbsp mild beer

salt and pepper

4 slices of bread

1 tbsp chopped fresh parsley, to garnish

cherry tomatoes, to serve

3

4

cook's tip

This is a variation of Welsh rarebit which does not traditionally contain chicken. Welsh rarebit topped with a poached egg is called buck rarebit.

1 Place the grated Wensleydale cheese, chicken, butter, Worcestershire sauce, mustard, plain flour and beer in a small saucepan. Mix all the ingredients together then season with salt and pepper to taste.

2 Gently bring the mixture to the boil then remove from the heat immediately.

3 Using a wooden spoon, beat until the mixture becomes creamy in texture. Allow the mixture to cool.

4 Once the chicken mixture has cooled, toast the bread on both sides and spread with the chicken mixture.

5 Place under a hot grill until bubbling and golden brown.

6 Garnish with a little chopped parsley and serve with cherry tomatoes.

chicken potato fritters

These fritters are delicious served with a green salad, a fresh vegetable salsa or a chilli sauce dip.

Makes 8

500 g/1 lb 2 oz mashed potato,
   with butter added

250 g/9 oz chopped, cooked chicken

125 g/4½ oz cooked ham, chopped finely

1 tbsp mixed herbs

2 eggs, lightly beaten

salt and pepper

milk

125 g/4½ oz fresh brown breadcrumbs

oil for shallow frying

sprig of fresh parsley, to garnish

mixed salad, to serve

1 In a large bowl, blend the potatoes, chicken, ham, herbs and 1 egg, and season well.

2 Shape the mixture into small balls or flat pancakes.

3 Add a little milk to the second egg.

4 Place the breadcrumbs on a plate. Dip the balls in the egg and milk mixture then roll in the breadcrumbs, to coat them completely.

5 Heat the cooking oil in a large frying pan and cook the fritters until they are golden brown. Garnish with a sprig of fresh parsley and serve with a mixed salad.

1

2

4

variation

A mixture of chopped fresh tarragon and parsley makes a fresh and flavourful addition to these fritters.

cook's tip

To make a tomato sauce to serve with the fritters, heat 200 ml/7 fl oz passata and 4 tbsp dry white wine. Season, remove from the heat and add 4 tbsp natural yogurt. Return to the heat and add chilli powder to taste.

mediterranean chicken with mixed peppers

All the sunshine colours and flavours of the Mediterranean are combined in this easy dish.

Serves 4

8 skinless chicken thighs

2 tbsp wholemeal flour

2 tbsp olive oil

1 small onion, sliced thinly

1 garlic clove, crushed

1 each large red, yellow and green peppers,
  sliced thinly

400 g/14 oz can chopped tomatoes

1 tbsp chopped oregano

salt and pepper

fresh oregano, to garnish

crusty wholemeal bread, to serve

1

3

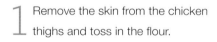

2

1 Remove the skin from the chicken thighs and toss in the flour.

2 Heat the oil in a wide pan and fry the chicken quickly until sealed and lightly browned, then remove from the pan. Add the onion to the pan and gently fry until soft. Add the garlic, peppers, tomatoes and oregano, then bring to the boil, stirring.

3 Arrange the chicken over the vegetables, season well with salt and pepper, then cover the pan tightly and simmer for 20–25 minutes or until the chicken is completely cooked and tender.

4 Season to taste, garnish with oregano and serve with crusty wholemeal bread.

cook's tip

If you do not have fresh oregano, use canned tomatoes with herbs already added.

variation

For extra flavour, halve the peppers and grill under a preheated grill until the skins are charred. Leave to cool then remove the skins and seeds. Slice the peppers thinly and use in the recipe.

open chicken sandwiches

These tasty sandwiches are good as a snack on their own or they can be served as part of a picnic spread.

3

Serves 6

6 thick slices of bread or a large French
    stick cut lengthways, then cut into 6
    pieces and buttered

3 hard-boiled eggs, the yolk sieved and the
    white chopped

25 g/1 oz butter, softened

2 tbsp English mustard

1 tsp anchovy essence

pepper

250 g/9 oz grated Cheddar cheese

3 cooked, skinless chicken breasts,
    chopped finely

12 slices each of tomato and cucumber

4

5

1 Remove the crusts from the bread
(optional).

2 Reserve the yolk and the white
separately from 1 egg.

3 In a large bowl, mix the remaining
egg with the softened butter,
English mustard and anchovy essence
and season well with pepper.

cook's tip

To soften butter, let it stand
at room temperature for 30
minutes or, if you are short
of time, cream it in a bowl
with a fork. Alternatively,
there are now varieties of
soft butter available from
supermarkets.

cook's tip

If you prefer a less spicy
flavour, use a milder mustard.
Add mayonnaise, if liked, and
garnish with watercress.

variation

Add 50 g/1¾ oz finely chopped
grilled bacon to the chicken
and cheese mixture for a
crunchier texture.

4 Mix in the grated Cheddar cheese
and chicken and spread the mixture
on the bread.

5 Make alternate rows of the egg yolk
and the egg white on top of the
chicken mixture. Arrange the tomato
and cucumber slices on top of the egg
and serve.

jacket potatoes with chicken & spring onions

Use the breasts from a roasted chicken for this delicious, healthy snack. Served with a mixed salad, it is an ideal light meal for a summer's day.

Serves 4

4 large baking potatoes

250 g/9 oz cooked, boneless
    chicken breasts

4 spring onions

250 g/9 oz low-fat soft cheese or Quark

pepper

coleslaw, green salad or a mixed salad,
    to serve

variation

For another delicious filling,
fry 250 g/9 oz button
mushrooms in a little butter.
Mix with the chicken then add
150 g/5½ oz natural yogurt,
1 tbsp tomato purée and 2 tsp
mild curry powder. Blend well
and use to fill the jackets.

cook's tip

Look for Quark in the chilled
section. It is a low-fat,
white, fresh curd cheese made
from cow's milk with a
delicate, slightly sour
flavour.

1 Scrub the potatoes and prick them all over with a fork. Bake in a preheated oven, 200°C/400°F/Gas Mark 6, for about 50 minutes until tender, or cook in a microwave on High/ 100% power for 12–15 minutes.

3

1

2 Using a sharp knife, dice the chicken, trim and thickly slice the spring onions and mix with the low-fat soft cheese or Quark.

3 Cut a cross through the top of each potato and pull slightly apart. Spoon the chicken filling into the potatoes and sprinkle with freshly ground black pepper. Serve immediately with coleslaw, green salad or a mixed salad.

2

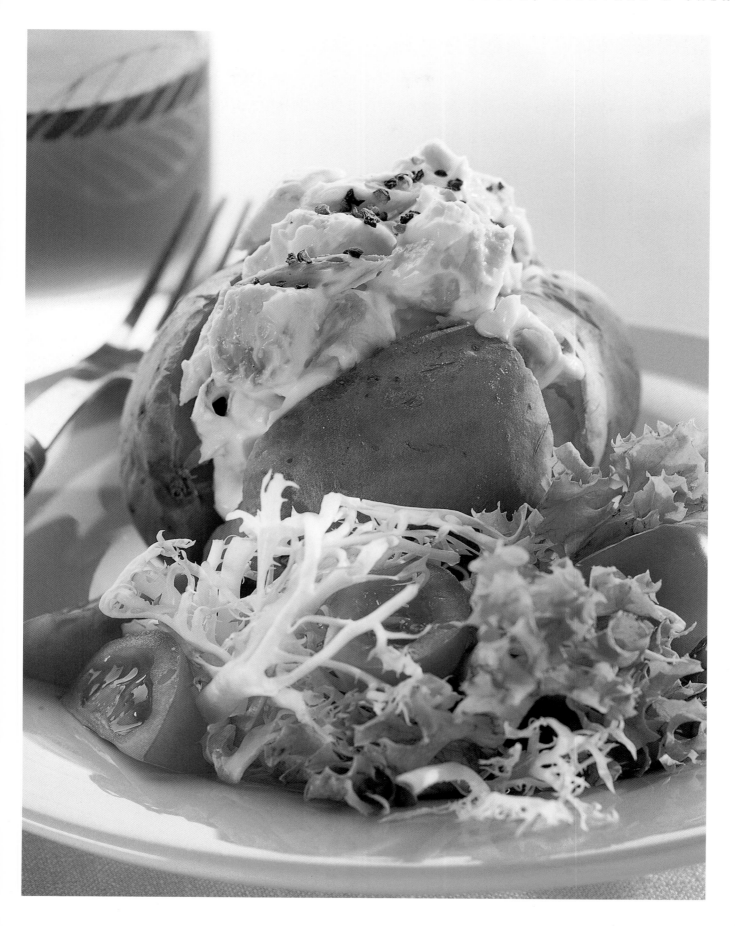

baked chicken pieces with rosemary

A very low-fat chicken recipe with a refreshingly light, mustard-spiced sauce, which is ideal for a healthy lunchbox or a light meal with salad.

Serves 4

25 g/1 oz rolled oats

1 tbsp chopped fresh rosemary

salt and pepper

4 skinless chicken quarters

1 egg white

150 g/5½ oz natural low-fat fromage frais

2 tsp wholegrain mustard

grated carrot salad, to serve

1

2

3

variation

To make oaty chicken nuggets, chop up 4 skinless, boneless chicken breasts into small pieces. Reduce the cooking time by about 10 minutes and test that the chicken is cooked. These nuggets would be ideal at a picnic, buffet or children's party.

variation

Add 1 tbsp sesame or sunflower seeds to the oat mixture for an even crunchier texture. Experiment with different herbs, instead of the rosemary.

1 Mix together the rolled oats, fresh rosemary and salt and pepper.

2 Brush each piece of chicken evenly with egg white, then coat in the oat mixture. Place on a baking sheet and bake in a preheated oven, 200°C/400°F/Gas Mark 6, for about 40 minutes or until the juices run clear when the chicken is pierced.

3 In a bowl, mix together the fromage frais and wholegrain mustard, season with salt and pepper to taste then serve with the chicken, hot or cold, with a grated carrot salad.

chicken livers with chilli & chinese cabbage

This is a richly flavoured dish with a dark, slightly tangy
sauce which is popular in China.

Serves 4

350 g/12 oz chicken livers

2 tbsp sunflower oil

1 red chilli, deseeded and finely chopped

1 tsp fresh grated ginger

2 cloves garlic, crushed

2 tbsp tomato ketchup

3 tbsp sherry

3 tbsp soy sauce

1 tsp cornflour

450 g/1 lb pak choi

egg noodles, to serve

1 Using a sharp knife, trim the fat from the chicken livers and slice into small pieces.

2 Heat the oil in a large wok. Add the chicken liver pieces and stir-fry over a high heat for 2–3 minutes.

3 Add the chilli, ginger and garlic and stir-fry for about 1 minute.

4 Mix together the tomato ketchup, sherry, soy sauce and cornflour in a small bowl and set aside.

5 Add the pak choi to the wok and stir-fry until it just wilts.

1

4

6 Add the reserved tomato ketchup mixture to the wok and cook, stirring to mix, until the juices start to bubble.

7 Transfer to serving bowls and serve hot with noodles.

5

cook's tip

Fresh ginger root will keep for several weeks in a dry, cool place.

cook's tip

Chicken livers are available fresh or frozen from most supermarkets.

mediterranean pan bagna

Perfect for a picnic or packed lunch, this Mediterranean-style sandwich can be prepared in advance.

Serves 6

1 large French stick

1 garlic clove

125 ml/4 fl oz olive oil

20 g/¾ oz canned anchovy fillets

50 g/2 oz cold roast chicken

2 large tomatoes, sliced

8 large, stoned black olives, chopped

pepper

1

2

5

1 Using a sharp bread knife, cut the French stick in half lengthways and open out.

2 Cut the garlic clove in half and rub over the bread.

3 Sprinkle the cut surface of the bread with the olive oil.

4 Drain the anchovies and set aside.

5 Thinly slice the chicken and arrange on top of the bread. Arrange the tomatoes and drained anchovies on top of the chicken.

6 Scatter with the chopped black olives and plenty of pepper. Sandwich the loaf back together and wrap tightly in foil until required. Cut into slices to serve.

variation

You could use Italian ciabatta or olive-studded focaccia bread instead of the French stick, if you prefer. The last few years have seen a growing interest in different breads and supermarkets now stock a wide range from home and abroad.

cook's tip

Arrange a few fresh basil leaves in between the tomato slices to add a warm, spicy flavour. Use a good quality olive oil in this recipe for extra flavour.

chicken liver & sage crostini

Crostini are small pieces of toast with a savoury topping. In Italy this is a popular antipasto dish.

Serves 4

2 tbsp olive oil

1 garlic clove, finely chopped

225 g/8 oz fresh or frozen chicken livers

2 tbsp white wine

2 tbsp lemon juice

4 fresh sage leaves, finely chopped or
  1 tsp dried, crumbled sage

salt and pepper

4 slices ciabatta or other Italian bread

wedges of lemon, to garnish

1 Heat the olive oil in a frying pan and cook the garlic for 1 minute.

2 Rinse and roughly chop the chicken livers, using a sharp knife.

3 Add the chicken liver to the frying pan together with the white wine and lemon juice. Cook for 3–4 minutes or until the juices from the chicken liver run clear.

4 Stir in the sage and season to taste with salt and pepper.

5 Under a preheated grill, toast the bread for 2 minutes on both sides or until golden-brown.

6 Spoon the hot chicken livers on top of the toasted bread and serve garnished with a wedge of lemon.

3

1

2

variation

Another way to make crostini is to slice a crusty loaf or a French loaf into small rounds or squares. Heat the olive oil in a frying pan and fry the slices of bread until golden brown and crisp on both sides. Remove the crostini from the pan with a perforated spoon and leave to drain on paper towels. Top with the chicken livers.

cook's tip

Overcooked liver is dry and tasteless. Cook the chopped liver for only 3-4 minutes — it should be soft and tender.

chicken pots with port

A food processor makes light work of blending
the ingredients for this recipe, but you can pound
by hand for a coarser mixture.

Serves 4-6

350 g/12 oz chopped smoked chicken

pinch each of grated nutmeg and mace

125 g/4½ oz butter, softened

2 tbsp port

2 tbsp double cream

salt and pepper

butter for clarifying (see Cook's Tip)

sprig of fresh parsley, to garnish

brown bread slices and fresh butter, to serve

cook's tip

This dish can be kept in the refrigerator for 2-3 days, but no longer as it does not contain any preservatives. It may be stored in the freezer for a maximum of 1 month.

2

4

5

cook's tip

To make clarified butter: place 250 g/9 oz butter in a saucepan and heat gently, skimming off the foam as the butter heats — the sediment will sink to the bottom of the pan. When the butter has completely melted, remove the pan from the heat and leave to stand for at least 4 minutes. Strain the butter through a piece of muslin into a bowl. Allow the butter to cool a little before spooning it over the surface of the potted chicken.

1 Place the smoked chicken in a large bowl with the remaining ingredients, and season with salt and pepper to taste.

2 Pound until the mixture is very smooth or blend in a food processor.

3 Transfer the mixture to individual earthenware pots or one large pot.

4 Cover each pot with buttered baking parchment and weigh down with cans or weights. Chill in the refrigerator for 4 hours.

5 Remove the parchment and cover with clarified butter (see Cook's Tip).

6 Garnish with a sprig of parsley and serve with slices of buttered brown bread.

chicken & spinach salad with ginger dressing

For this simple, refreshing summer salad you can use leftover roast chicken, or ready-roasted chicken to save time. Add the dressing just before serving, or the spinach will lose its crispness.

Serves 4

250 g/9 oz young spinach leaves

3 sticks celery, sliced thinly

½ cucumber

2 spring onions

3 tbsp chopped fresh parsley

350g/12 oz boneless,
    roast chicken, sliced thinly

DRESSING

2.5 cm/1 inch piece fresh ginger root,
    grated finely

3 tbsp olive oil

1 tbsp white wine vinegar

1 tbsp clear honey

½ tsp ground cinnamon

salt and pepper

smoked almonds, to garnish (optional)

2

3

4

variation

Substitute lamb's lettuce for the spinach, if you prefer.

cook's tip

Fresh young spinach leaves go particularly well with fruit — try adding a few fresh raspberries or nectarine slices to make an even more refreshing salad.

1 Thoroughly wash the spinach leaves, then pat dry with paper towels.

2 Using a sharp knife, thinly slice the celery, cucumber and spring onions. Toss in a large bowl with the spinach leaves and parsley.

3 Transfer to serving plates and arrange the chicken on top of the salad.

4 In a screw-topped jar, combine all the dressing ingredients and shake well to mix. Season the dressing with salt and pepper to taste, then pour over the salad. Garnish with a few smoked almonds, if using.

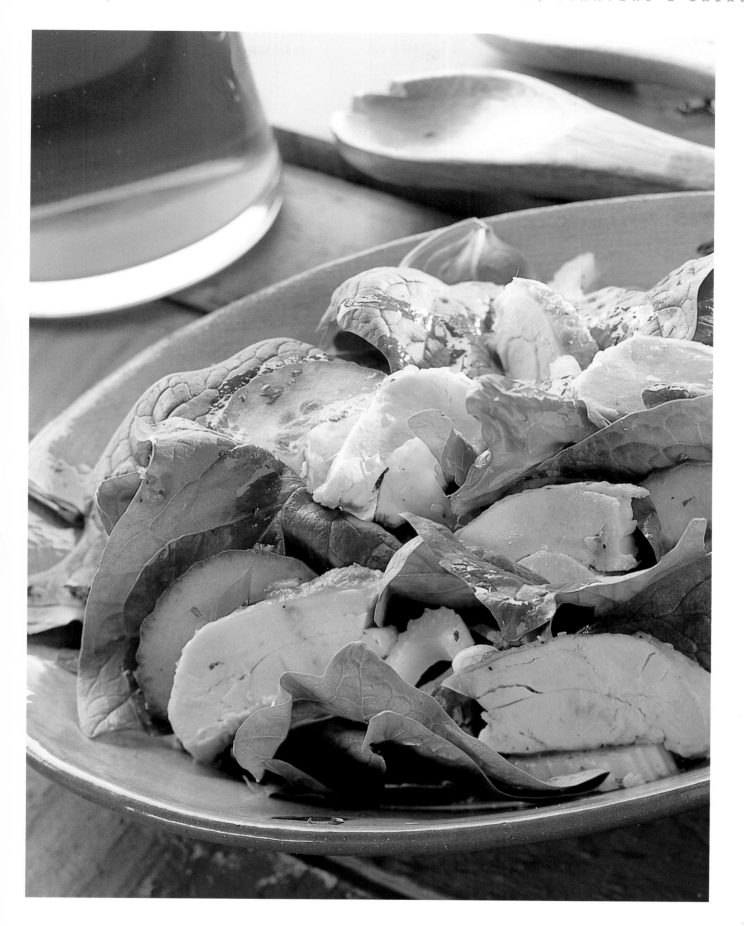

classic chicken salad with saffron rice

This classic salad is good as a starter or as part of a buffet. Mango chutney makes a tasty addition.

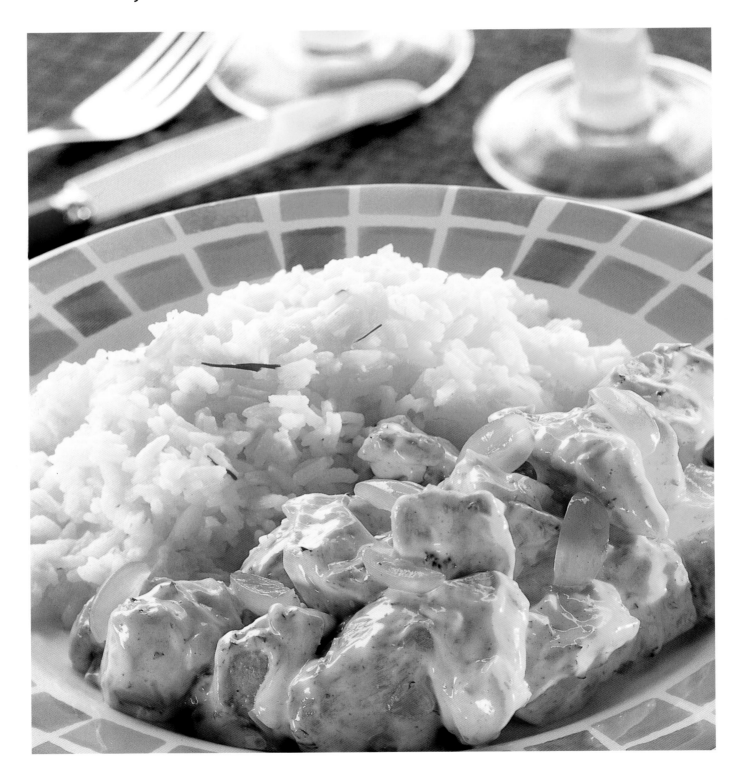

Serves 6

4 tbsp olive oil

900 g/2 lb chicken meat, diced

125 g/4½ oz rindless, smoked bacon, diced

12 shallots

2 garlic cloves, crushed

1 tbsp mild curry powder

pepper

300 ml/½ pint mayonnaise

1 tbsp clear honey

1 tbsp chopped fresh parsley

90 g/3 oz seedless black grapes, quartered,
    to garnish

cold saffron rice, to serve

1 Heat the oil in a large frying pan and add the chicken, bacon, shallots, garlic and curry powder. Cook slowly for about 15 minutes.

2 Spoon the mixture into a clean mixing bowl.

3 Allow the mixture to cool completely then season with pepper to taste.

cook's tip

You can use this recipe to fill a jacket potato or as a sandwich filling, but cut the chicken into smaller pieces.

4 Blend the mayonnaise with a little honey to taste, then add the chopped fresh parsley. Toss the chicken in the mixture.

5 Place the mixture in a deep serving dish, garnish with the grapes and serve with cold saffron rice.

1

4

4

variation

Add 2 tbsp chopped fresh apricots and 2 tbsp flaked almonds to the sauce in step 4. For a healthier version of this dish, replace the mayonnaise with the same quantity of natural yogurt and omit the honey, otherwise the sauce will be too runny.

lemon chicken & walnut salad

This colourful and healthy dish is a variation of a classic salad. Served with crusty brown rolls, it is an ideal light meal for a summer's day

Serves 4

500 g/1 lb 2 oz red apples, diced

3 tbsp fresh lemon juice

150 ml/¼ pint light mayonnaise

1 head of celery

4 shallots, sliced

1 garlic clove, crushed

90 g/3 oz walnuts, chopped

500 g/1 lb 2 oz cooked chicken, cubed

1 cos lettuce

pepper

sliced apple and walnuts, to garnish

cook's tip

Soaking the apples in lemon juice prevents discoloration.

variation

Instead of the shallots, use spring onions for a milder flavour. Trim the spring onions and slice finely.

1

2

4

3 Add the celery, shallots, garlic and walnuts to the apple and mix together.

4 Stir in the mayonnaise and blend thoroughly.

5 Add the cooked chicken to the bowl and mix well.

6 Line a glass salad bowl or serving dish with the lettuce leaves. Pile the chicken salad into the centre, sprinkle with pepper and garnish with the apple slices and walnuts.

1 Place the apples in a bowl with the lemon juice and 1 tablespoon of mayonnaise. Leave for 40 minutes.

2 Using a sharp knife, slice the celery very thinly.

chicken & herring platter

This recipe is ideally suited as a cold platter for a buffet party or a spectacular starter for a special meal.

Serves 4

1 large lettuce

4 chicken breasts, cooked and sliced thinly

8 rollmop herrings and their marinade

6 hard-boiled eggs, quartered

125 g/4½ oz cooked ham, sliced

125 g/4½ oz roast beef, sliced

125 g/4½ oz roast lamb, sliced

150 g/5½ oz mangetout, cooked

125 g/4½ oz seedless black grapes,

20 stuffed olives, sliced

12 shallots, boiled

60 g/2 oz flaked almonds

60 g/2 oz sultanas

2 oranges

sprig of mint

salt and pepper

fresh crusty bread, to serve

1 Spread out the lettuce leaves on a large oval platter.

2 Arrange the chicken in three sections on the platter.

3 Place the rollmops, eggs and meats in lines or sections over the remainder of the platter.

4 Use the mangetout, grapes, olives, shallots, almonds and sultanas to fill in the spaces between the sections.

5 Grate the rind from the oranges and sprinkle over the whole platter. Peel and slice the oranges and add the orange slices and mint sprig to the platter. Season well with salt and pepper. Sprinkle with the herring marinade and serve with crusty bread.

variation

Should you wish, serve with cold, cooked vegetables, such as sliced beans, baby sweetcorn and cooked beetroot.

2

1

3

warm chicken & rice salad

The sweetness of the pears complements perfectly the sharp taste of the blue cheese in this delicious warm salad.

Serves 6

50 ml/2 fl oz olive oil

6 shallots, sliced

1 garlic clove, crushed

2 tbsp chopped fresh tarragon

1 tbsp English mustard

salt and pepper

6 skinless, boneless chicken breasts

1 tbsp flour

150 ml/¼ pint chicken stock

1 apple, diced finely

1 tbsp chopped walnuts

2 tbsp double cream

SALAD

250 g/9 oz cooked rice

2 large pears, diced

150 g/5½ oz blue cheese, diced

1 red pepper, diced

1 tbsp chopped fresh coriander

1 tbsp sesame oil

1

2

4

1 Place the olive oil, shallots, garlic, tarragon and mustard in a deep bowl. Season well and mix the ingredients together thoroughly.

2 Place the chicken in the marinade to coat completely, cover with clingfilm and chill in the refrigerator for about 4 hours.

3 Drain the chicken, reserving the marinade. Quickly fry the chicken in a large, deep non-stick frying pan for 4 minutes on both sides. Transfer the chicken to a warm serving dish.

4 Add the marinade to the pan, bring to the boil and sprinkle with the flour. Add the chicken stock, apple and walnuts and gently simmer for 5 minutes. Return the chicken to the sauce, add the double cream and cook for 2 minutes.

5 Mix the salad ingredients together, place a little on each plate and top with a chicken breast and a spoonful of the sauce.

One of the marvellous qualities of chicken is that when it is cut into small pieces, it can be cooked very quickly, which is welcome for those of us who are too busy to spend a lot of time preparing meals. In this section, you can select a tasty nutritious dish that won't take hours to make. Pasta makes a perfect partner for chicken as it is also quick to cook — Chicken Fusilli look impressive and will fool guests into thinking that you have spent hours slaving away in the kitchen.

Chicken breasts are cooked with a delicious basil, hazelnut and garlic filling and then served on a bed of pasta, olives and sun-dried tomatoes. Smaller cuts of chicken are also ideal for stir-fries that can be quickly cooked to produce tender, moist and flavourful chicken. Peanut Chicken with Thread

Noodles is a crunchy stir-fry that is served with noodles. Risottos are also an excellent choice for when you are in a hurry – this chapter contains two risotto recipes although the variations for risotto are endless!

speedy meals

chinese chop suey with chicken & leek

Both well known and popular, chop suey dishes are easy to make and delicious. They are based on beansprouts and soy sauce with a meat or vegetable flavouring.

Serves 4

4 tbsp light soy sauce

2 tsp light brown sugar

500 g/1¼ lb skinless, boneless chicken
    breasts

3 tbsp vegetable oil

2 onions, quartered

2 garlic cloves, crushed

350 g/12 oz beansprouts

3 tsp sesame oil

1 tbsp cornflour

3 tbsp water

425 ml/¾ pint chicken stock

shredded leek, to garnish

1 Mix the soy sauce and sugar together, stirring until the sugar has dissolved.

2 Trim any fat from the chicken and cut the meat into thin strips. Place the chicken strips in a shallow glass dish and spoon the soy mixture over them, turning to coat. Leave to marinate in the refrigerator for 20 minutes.

3 Heat the oil in a preheated wok. Add the chicken and stir-fry for 2–3 minutes, until golden brown.

4 Add the onions and garlic and cook for a further 2 minutes. Add the beansprouts, cook for a further 4–5 minutes, then add the sesame oil.

5 Blend the cornflour with the water to form a smooth paste. Pour the stock into the wok, together with the cornflour paste and bring to the boil, stirring constantly until the sauce is thickened and clear. Transfer to a warm serving dish, garnish with shredded leek and serve immediately.

variation

This recipe may be made with strips of lean steak, pork or with mixed vegetables. Change the type of stock accordingly.

2

3

4

chicken & aubergine stir-fry

This is a delicious curried chicken and aubergine dish, flavoured with tomatoes and seasoned with fresh mint.

5

Serves 4

5 tbsp sunflower oil

2 cloves garlic, crushed

1 tbsp cumin seeds

1 tbsp mild curry powder

1 tbsp paprika

450 g/1 lb boneless, skinless chicken
  breasts

1 large aubergine, cubed

4 tomatoes, cut into quarters

100 ml/3½ fl oz chicken stock

1 tbsp fresh lemon juice

½ tsp salt

150 ml/¼ pint natural yogurt

1 tbsp chopped fresh mint

1 Heat 2 tablespoons of the sunflower
oil in a large preheated wok.

2 Add the garlic, cumin seeds, curry
powder and paprika to the wok and
stir-fry for 1 minute.

3 Using a sharp knife, thinly slice the
chicken breasts.

4 Add the rest of the oil to the wok
and stir-fry the chicken for 5
minutes.

2

4

5 Add the aubergine cubes, tomatoes
and chicken stock and bring to the
boil. Reduce the heat and leave to
simmer for about 20 minutes.

6 Stir in the lemon juice, salt and
yogurt and cook over a gentle
heat for a further 5 minutes, stirring
occasionally.

7 Scatter with chopped fresh mint
and transfer to serving bowls.
Serve immediately.

cook's tip

Once the yogurt has been
added, do not boil the sauce
as the yogurt will curdle.

stir-fried chicken & cashew nuts

Yellow bean sauce is made from yellow soy beans and is available in most supermarkets. Try to buy a chunky sauce rather than a smooth sauce for texture.

3

Serves 4

2 tbsp sunflower oil

450 g/1 lb skinless, boneless
    chicken breasts

2 cloves garlic, crushed

1 green pepper

100 g/3½ oz mangetout

6 spring onions, sliced, plus extra to garnish

225 g/8 oz spring greens or cabbage,
    shredded

160 g/5¾ oz jar yellow bean sauce

50 g/1¾ oz roasted cashew nuts

4

5

cook's tip

Do not add salted cashew nuts
to this dish, combined with
the slightly salty sauce,
the dish will be very salty
indeed.

1 Heat the sunflower oil in a large
  preheated wok.

2 Using a sharp knife, slice the
  chicken into thin strips.

3 Add the chicken to the wok
  together with the garlic. Stir-fry for
about 5 minutes or until the chicken is
sealed on all sides and beginning to
turn golden.

4 Using a sharp knife, deseed the
  green pepper and cut into
thin strips.

5 Add the mangetout, spring onions,
  green pepper strips and spring
greens or cabbage to the wok. Stir-fry
for a further 5 minutes or until the
vegetables are just tender.

6 Stir in the yellow bean sauce and
  heat through for about 2 minutes
or until the mixture starts to bubble.

7 Scatter with the roasted
  cashew nuts.

8 Transfer the chicken, spring green
  and yellow bean stir-fry to warm
serving plates and garnish with extra
spring onions, if desired. Serve the
stir-fry immediately.

chicken & green pepper stir-fry

Crushed mixed peppercorns coat tender, thin strips of chicken which are cooked with green and red peppers for a really colourful dish.

Serves 4

2 tbsp tomato ketchup

2 tbsp soy sauce

450 g/1 lb boneless, skinless chicken
    breasts

2 tbsp crushed mixed peppercorns

2 tbsp sunflower oil

1 red pepper

1 green pepper

175 g/6 oz sugar snap peas

2 tbsp oyster sauce

variation

Use mangetout instead of sugar snap peas, if you prefer.

1

2

1 Mix the tomato ketchup with the soy sauce in a bowl.

2 Using a sharp knife, slice the chicken into thin strips. Toss the chicken in the tomato ketchup and soy sauce mixture.

3 Sprinkle the crushed peppercorns on to a plate. Dip the coated chicken in the peppercorns until evenly coated.

4 Heat the sunflower oil in a preheated wok.

5 Add the chicken to the wok and stir-fry for 5 minutes.

6 Deseed and slice the peppers.

7 Add the peppers to the wok together with the sugar snap peas and stir-fry for a further 5 minutes.

8 Add the oyster sauce and allow to bubble for 2 minutes. Transfer to serving bowls and serve immediately.

6

sherried chicken & orange stir-fry with chives

The oranges add colour and piquancy to this refreshing dish, which complements the chicken well.

Serves 4

2 tbsp sunflower oil

1 onion, sliced

175 g/6 oz carrots, cut into thin sticks

1 clove garlic, crushed

350 g/12 oz boneless skinless chicken
   breasts

2 tbsp fresh ginger, peeled and grated

1 tsp ground ginger

4 tbsp sweet sherry

1 tbsp tomato purée

1 tbsp demerara sugar

100 ml/3½ fl oz orange juice

1 tsp cornflour

1 orange, peeled and segmented

fresh snipped chives, to garnish

cook's tip

Make sure that you do not
continue cooking the dish once
the orange segments have been
added in step 4, otherwise
they will break up.

1

2

3

1 Heat the oil in a large preheated
wok. Add the onion, carrots and
garlic and stir-fry over a high heat for
3 minutes or until the vegetables begin
to soften.

2 Using a sharp knife, slice the
chicken into thin strips. Add the
chicken to the wok together with the
fresh ginger and ground ginger. Stir-fry
for a further 10 minutes, or until the
chicken is well cooked through and
golden in colour.

3 Mix together the sherry, tomato
purée, sugar, orange juice and
cornflour in a bowl. Stir the mixture into
the wok and heat through until the
mixture bubbles and the juices start
to thicken.

4 Add the orange segments and
carefully toss to mix.

5 Transfer the stir-fried chicken to
warm serving bowls and garnish
with freshly snipped chives. Serve
immediately.

chinese sweet chicken with mixed vegetables

Clear honey is often added to Chinese recipes for sweetness. It combines well with the saltiness of the soy sauce.

Serves 4

2 tbsp clear honey

3 tbsp light soy sauce

1 tsp Chinese five-spice powder

1 tbsp sweet sherry

1 clove garlic, crushed

8 chicken thighs

1 tbsp sunflower oil

1 red chilli

100 g/3½ oz baby sweetcorns, halved

8 spring onions, sliced

150 g/5½ oz beansprouts

cook's tip

Chinese five-spice powder is found in most large supermarkets and is a blend of aromatic spices.

1 Mix together the honey, soy sauce, Chinese five-spice powder, sherry and garlic in a large bowl.

2 Using a sharp knife, make 3 slashes in the skin of each chicken thigh. Brush the honey and soy marinade over the chicken thighs, cover and leave to stand for at least 30 minutes.

3 Heat the oil in a large preheated wok.

4 Add the chicken to the wok and cook over a fairly high heat for 12–15 minutes, or until the chicken browns and the skin begins to crisp. Remove the chicken with a slotted spoon.

5 Using a sharp knife, deseed and very finely chop the chilli.

6 Add the chilli, sweetcorn, spring onions and beansprouts to the wok and stir-fry for 5 minutes.

7 Return the chicken to the wok and mix all of the ingredients together until completely heated through.

8 Transfer to serving plates and serve immediately.

1

2

5

chicken & mushrooms with yellow bean sauce

Chicken and cashew nuts are a great classic combination, as in this recipe. Flavoured with yellow bean sauce it is a quick and delicious dish.

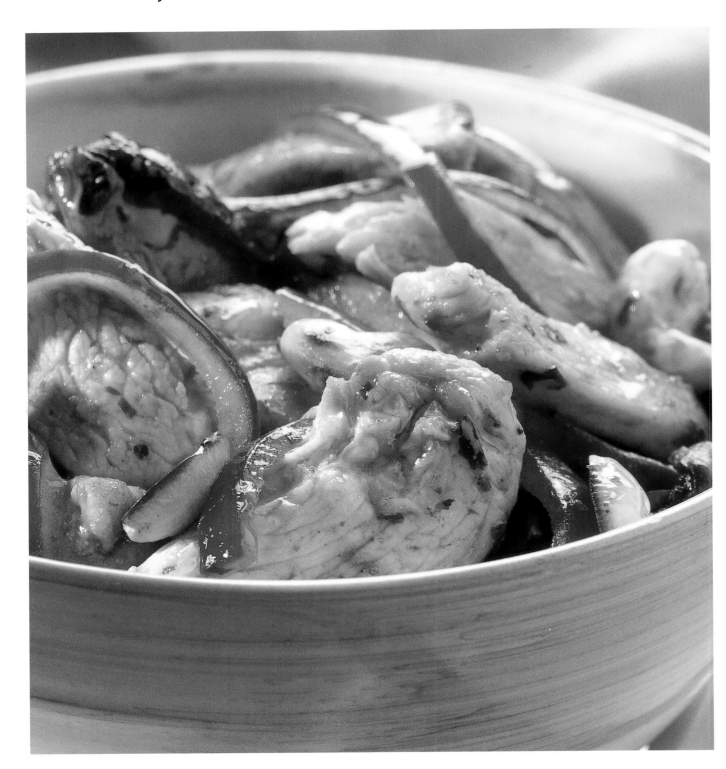

Serves 4

450 g/1 lb boneless chicken breasts

2 tbsp vegetable oil

1 red onion, sliced

175 g/6 oz flat mushrooms, sliced

100 g/3½ oz cashew nuts

75 g/2¾ oz jar yellow bean sauce

fresh coriander, to garnish

egg fried rice or plain boiled rice, to serve

1 Using a sharp knife, remove the excess skin from the chicken breasts if desired. Cut the chicken into small, bite-sized chunks.

2 Heat the vegetable oil in a preheated wok.

3 Add the chicken to the wok and stir-fry for 5 minutes.

1

3

4

4 Add the red onion and mushrooms to the wok and continue to stir-fry for a further 5 minutes.

5 Place the cashew nuts on a baking tray and toast under a preheated medium grill until just browning – this brings out their flavour.

6 Toss the toasted cashew nuts into the wok together with the yellow bean sauce. Allow the sauce to bubble for 2–3 minutes.

7 Transfer to warm serving bowls and garnish with fresh coriander. Serve hot with egg fried rice or plain boiled rice.

cook's tip

Chicken thighs could be used instead of the chicken breasts for a more economical dish.

chicken stir-fry with cumin & chinese cabbage

Cumin seeds are more frequently associated with Indian cooking, but they are used in this Chinese recipe for their earthy flavour. You could use ¹/₂ tsp of ground cumin instead.

Serves 4

450 g/1 lb boneless, skinless chicken
  breasts

2 tbsp sunflower oil

1 clove garlic, crushed

1 tbsp cumin seeds

1 tbsp grated fresh ginger root

1 red chilli, deseeded and sliced

1 red pepper, deseeded and sliced

1 green pepper, deseeded and sliced

1 yellow pepper, deseeded and sliced

100 g/3½ oz beansprouts

350 g/12 oz pak choi or other green leaves

2 tbsp sweet chilli sauce

3 tbsp light soy sauce

deep-fried crispy ginger, to garnish (see
  Cook's Tip)

1 Using a sharp knife, slice the chicken breasts into thin strips.

2 Heat the oil in a large preheated wok.

3 Add the chicken to the wok and stir-fry for 5 minutes.

4 Add the garlic, cumin seeds, ginger and chilli to the wok, stirring to mix.

5 Add all of the peppers to the wok and stir-fry for a further 5 minutes.

6 Toss in the beansprouts and pak choi together with the sweet chilli sauce and soy sauce and continue to cook until the pak choi leaves start to wilt.

6

7 Transfer to warm serving bowls and garnish with deep-fried ginger (see Cook's Tip).

4

5

cook's tip

To make the deep-fried crispy ginger garnish, peel and thinly slice a large piece of root ginger, using a sharp knife. Carefully lower the slices of ginger into a wok or small pan of hot oil and cook for about 30 seconds. Remove the deep-fried ginger with a slotted spoon, transfer to sheets of absorbent kitchen paper and leave to drain thoroughly.

chicken, leek & mango stir-fry

This is quite a sweet dish as mango has a sweet, scented flavour.

2

Serves 4

1 tbsp sunflower oil

6 skinless, boneless chicken thighs

1 ripe mango

2 cloves garlic, crushed

225 g/8 oz leeks, shredded

100 g/3½ oz beansprouts

150 ml/¼ pint mango juice

1 tbsp white wine vinegar

2 tbsp clear honey

2 tbsp tomato ketchup

1 tsp cornflour

4

cook's tip

Mango juice is available in jars from most supermarkets and is quite thick and sweet. If unavailable, purée and sieve a ripe mango and add a little water to make up the required quantity.

1 Heat the sunflower oil in a large preheated wok.

2 Using a sharp knife, cut the chicken into bite-sized cubes.

3 Add the chicken to the wok and stir-fry over a high heat for 10 minutes, tossing frequently until the chicken is cooked through and golden in colour.

4 Meanwhile, peel and slice the mango.

5 Add the garlic, leeks, mango and beansprouts to the wok and stir-fry for a further 2–3 minutes, or until softened.

6 Mix together the mango juice, white wine vinegar, clear honey and tomato ketchup with the cornflour in a measuring jug.

7 Pour the mango juice and cornflour mixture into the wok and stir-fry for a further 2 minutes, or until the juices start to thicken.

8 Transfer to a warmed serving dish and serve immediately.

6

curried chicken with sweet potato

This is a really colourful dish, the red of the tomatoes
perfectly complementing the orange sweet potato.

Serves 4

1 tbsp sunflower oil

450 g/1 lb boneless, skinless chicken

2 cloves garlic, crushed

2 tbsp Thai red curry paste

2 tbsp fresh grated galangal or root ginger

1 tbsp tamarind paste

4 lime leaves

225 g/8 oz sweet potato

600 ml/1 pint coconut milk

225 g/8 oz cherry tomatoes, halved

3 tbsp chopped fresh coriander

cooked jasmine or Thai fragrant rice, to serve

1 Heat the sunflower oil in a large preheated wok.

2 Thinly slice the chicken. Add the chicken to the wok and stir-fry for 5 minutes.

3 Add the garlic, curry paste, galangal or root ginger, tamarind and lime leaves to the wok and stir-fry for 1 minute.

3

5

4

4 Using a sharp knife, peel and dice the sweet potato.

5 Add the coconut milk and sweet potato to the mixture in the wok and bring to the boil. Allow to bubble

over a medium heat for 20 minutes, or until the juices start to thicken and reduce.

6 Add the cherry tomatoes and coriander to the curry and cook for a further 5 minutes, stirring occasionally. Transfer to serving plates and serve hot with cooked jasmine or Thai fragrant rice.

cook's tip

Galangal is a spice very similar to ginger and is used to replace the latter in Thai cuisine. It can be bought fresh from Oriental food stores but is also available dried and as a powder. The fresh root, which is not as pungent as ginger, needs to be peeled before slicing to use.

sesame chicken with lemon curd

Sesame seeds have a strong flavour which adds nuttiness to recipes.
They are perfect for coating these thin chicken strips.

Serves 4

4 boneless, skinless chicken breasts

1 egg white

25 g/1 oz sesame seeds

2 tbsp vegetable oil

1 onion, sliced

1 tbsp demerara sugar

finely grated zest and juice of
   1 lemon

3 tbsp lemon curd

200 g/7 oz can waterchestnuts

lemon zest, to garnish

cook's tip

Waterchestnuts are commonly
added to Chinese recipes
purely for their crunchy
texture as they do not have
a great deal of flavour.

1 Place the chicken breasts between 2 sheets of clingfilm and pound with a rolling pin to flatten. Slice the chicken into thin strips.

2 Whisk the egg white until light and foamy.

3 Dip the chicken strips into the egg white, then into the sesame seeds until coated evenly.

1

3

4 Heat the oil in a large preheated wok.

5 Add the onion to the wok and stir-fry until just softened.

6 Add the sesame-coated chicken to the wok and continue stir-frying for 5 minutes, or until the chicken turns golden.

7 Mix together the sugar, lemon zest, lemon juice and the lemon curd and add the mixture to the wok. Allow the lemon mixture to bubble slightly without stirring.

8 Drain the waterchestnuts and slice them thinly, using a sharp knife. Add the waterchestnuts to the wok and heat through for 2 minutes. Transfer to serving bowls, garnish with lemon zest and serve hot.

8

sherried chicken stir-fry

Chicken thighs are inexpensive, meaty portions of the chicken which are readily available. The meat is not as tender as the breast but it is perfect for stir-frying.

Serves 4

3 tbsp sunflower oil

350 g/12 oz boneless chicken thighs,
  skinned and cut into thin strips

1 onion, sliced

1 clove garlic, crushed

1 red pepper, deseeded and sliced

75 g/2¾ oz mangetout

4 tbsp light soy sauce

4 tbsp sherry

1 tbsp tomato purée

finely grated rind and juice of 1 orange

1 tsp cornflour

2 oranges

100 g/3½ oz beansprouts

cooked rice or noodles, to serve

cook's tip

Beansprouts are sprouting mung beans and are a regular ingredient in Chinese cooking. They require very little cooking and may even be eaten raw, if wished.

2

1 Heat the sunflower oil in a large preheated wok.

2 Add the strips of chicken to the wok and stir-fry for 2–3 minutes or until sealed on all sides.

3 Add the sliced onion, garlic, pepper and mangetout to the wok. Stir-fry the mixture for a further 5 minutes, or until the vegetables are just becoming tender and the chicken is completely cooked through.

4 Mix together the soy sauce, sherry, tomato purée, orange rind and juice and the cornflour in a measuring jug.

5 Add the mixture to the wok and cook, stirring, until the juices start to thicken.

6 Using a sharp knife, peel and segment the oranges.

7 Add the orange segments and beansprouts to the mixture in the wok and heat through for a further 2 minutes.

8 Transfer the stir-fry to serving plates and serve at once with cooked rice or noodles.

4

6

caramelised chicken breasts

This quick and healthy dish is stir-fried, which means you need use only the minimum of fat. If you don't have a wok, use a wide frying pan instead.

1

Serves 4

4 skinless, boneless chicken breasts

250 g/9 oz baby sweetcorn

250 g/9 oz mangetout

2 tbsp sunflower oil

1 tbsp sherry vinegar

1 tbsp honey

1 tbsp light soy sauce

1 tbsp sunflower seeds

pepper

rice or egg noodles, to serve

3

4

1 Using a sharp knife, slice the chicken breasts into long, thin strips. Cut the baby sweetcorn in half lengthways and top and tail the mangetout. Set the vegetables aside until required.

2 Heat the sunflower oil in a wok or a wide frying pan and fry the chicken over a fairly high heat, stirring constantly, for 1 minute.

3 Add the corn and mangetout and stir over a moderate heat for 5–8 minutes, until evenly cooked.

4 Mix together the sherry vinegar, honey and soy sauce and stir into the pan with the sunflower seeds. Season with pepper to taste. Cook, stirring constantly, for 1 minute. Serve hot with rice or Chinese egg noodles.

cook's tip

Rice vinegar or balsamic vinegar makes a good substitute for the sherry vinegar.

stir-fried garlic chicken with coriander & lime

Garlic and coriander butter flavours and moistens chicken breasts which are served with a caramelised sauce, sharpened with lime juice.

Serves 4

4 large skinless, boneless chicken breasts

50 g/1¾ oz garlic butter, softened

3 tbsp chopped fresh coriander

1 tbsp sunflower oil

finely grated zest and juice of 2 limes

25 g/1 oz palm sugar or demerara sugar

coriander, to garnish (optional)

boiled rice, to serve

cook's tip

Be sure to check that the chicken is cooked through before slicing and serving. Cook over a gentle heat so as not to overcook the outside, but ensuring the middle is cooked.

1 Place each chicken breast between 2 sheets of clingfilm and pound with a rolling pin until flattened to about 1 cm/½ inch thick.

2 Mix together the garlic butter and coriander and spread over each flattened chicken breast. Roll up like a Swiss roll and secure with cocktail sticks.

3

2

2

3 Heat the oil in a wok. Add the chicken rolls and cook, turning, for 15–20 minutes or until cooked through.

4 Remove the chicken from the wok and transfer to a board. Cut each chicken roll into slices.

5 Add the lime zest, juice and sugar to the wok and heat gently, stirring, until the sugar has dissolved. Raise the heat and allow to bubble for 2 minutes.

6 Arrange the chicken on warmed serving plates and spoon the pan juices over to serve.

7 Garnish with extra coriander if desired.

peanut chicken with thread noodles

A complete main course cooked within ten minutes. Thread egg noodles are the ideal accompaniment because they can be cooked quickly and easily while the stir-fry sizzles.

Serves 4

300 g/10½ oz courgettes

250 g/9 oz baby sweetcorn

300 g/10½ oz button mushrooms

250 g/9 oz thread egg noodles

2 tbsp corn oil

1 tbsp sesame oil

8 boneless chicken thighs
    or 4 breasts, sliced thinly

350 g/12 oz beansprouts

4 tbsp smooth peanut butter

2 tbsp soy sauce

2 tbsp lime or lemon juice

60 g/2 oz roasted peanuts

pepper

coriander, to garnish

1

3

4

1 Using a sharp knife, trim and thinly slice the courgettes, sweetcorn and button mushrooms.

2 Bring a large pan of lightly salted boiling water to the boil and cook the noodles for 3–4 minutes. Meanwhile, heat the corn oil and sesame oil in a large frying pan or wok and fry the chicken over a fairly high heat for 1 minute.

3 Add the sliced courgettes, sweetcorn and button mushrooms and stir-fry for 5 minutes.

4 Add the beansprouts, peanut butter, soy sauce, lime or lemon juice and pepper, then cook for a further 2 minutes.

5 Drain the noodles, transfer to a serving dish and scatter with the peanuts. Serve with the stir-fried chicken and vegetables, garnished with a sprig of fresh coriander.

cook's tip

Try serving this stir-fry with rice sticks. These are broad, pale, translucent ribbon noodles made from ground rice.

chicken & okra curry

Okra or ladies fingers are slightly bitter in flavour. The pineapple and coconut in this recipe offsets them in both colour and flavour.

Serves 4

2 tbsp sunflower oil or 25 g/1 oz ghee

450 g/1 lb boneless, skinless chicken thighs
   or breasts

150 g/5½ oz okra

1 large onion, sliced

2 cloves garlic, crushed

3 tbsp mild curry paste

300 ml/½ pint chicken stock

1 tbsp fresh lemon juice

100 g/3½ oz creamed coconut

175 g/6 oz fresh or canned pineapple,
   cubed

150 ml/¼ pint thick natural yogurt

2 tbsp chopped fresh coriander

lemon wedges and fresh coriander sprigs,
   to garnish

freshly boiled rice, to serve

1 Heat the sunflower oil or ghee in a large preheated wok.

2 Using a sharp knife, cut the chicken into bite-sized pieces. Add the chicken to the wok and cook, stirring frequently, until evenly browned.

3 Using a sharp knife, trim the okra.

4 Add the onion, garlic and okra to the wok and cook for a further 2–3 minutes, stirring constantly.

5 Mix the curry paste with the chicken stock and lemon juice and pour over the mixture in the wok. Bring to the boil, cover and leave to simmer for 30 minutes.

6 Coarsley grate the creamed coconut, stir it into the curry and cook for about 5 minutes – the creamed coconut will help to thicken the juices.

7 Add the pineapple, yogurt and coriander and heat through for 2 minutes, stirring.

8 Garnish with lemon wedges and coriander and serve hot with boiled rice.

2

3

5

cook's tip

Score around the top of the okra with a knife before cooking to release the sticky glue-like substance which is bitter in taste.

chilli & basil drumsticks

Chicken drumsticks are cooked in a delicious sauce and served with deep-fried basil for colour and flavour.

Serves 4

8 chicken drumsticks

2 tbsp soy sauce

1 tbsp sunflower oil

1 red chilli

100 g/3½ oz carrots, cut into thin sticks

6 celery stalks, cut into sticks

3 tbsp sweet chilli sauce

oil, for frying

about 50 fresh basil leaves

1 Remove the skin from the chicken drumsticks, if desired. Make 3 slashes in each drumstick. Brush the drumsticks with the soy sauce.

2 Heat the oil in a preheated wok and fry the drumsticks for 20 minutes, turning frequently, until they are cooked through.

3 Deseed and finely chop the chilli. Add the chilli, carrots and celery to the wok and cook for a further 5 minutes. Stir in the chilli sauce, cover and allow to bubble gently whilst preparing the basil leaves.

4 Heat a little oil in a heavy based pan. Carefully add the basil leaves (stand well away from the pan and protect your hand with a tea towel as they may spit a little). Cook for about 30 seconds or until they begin to curl up but not brown. Transfer to kitchen paper to drain.

5 Arrange the cooked chicken, vegetables and pan juices on to a warm serving plate and garnish with the deep-fried crispy basil leaves.

1

3

1

cook's tip

Basil has a very strong flavour which is perfect with chicken and Chinese flavourings. You could use baby spinach instead of the basil, if you prefer.

crispy-coated chicken morsels

Served with a smooth creamy tomato sauce, this makes an excellent light lunch with freshly baked cheese bread.

Serves 4-6

175 g/6 oz fresh breadcrumbs

250 g/9 oz cooked chicken, minced

1 small leek, chopped finely

pinch each of mixed herbs and mustard
   powder

salt and pepper

2 eggs, separated

4 tbsp milk

crisp breadcrumbs, for coating

25 g/1 oz beef dripping

cook's tip

Make your own minced chicken by working lean cuts of chicken in a food processor.

variation

If you want to lower the saturated fat content of this recipe, use a little oil for frying instead of the dripping.

1 In a large clean bowl, combine the breadcrumbs, minced chicken, leek, mixed herbs and mustard powder, and season with salt and pepper. Mix together until thoroughly incorporated.

2 Add 1 whole egg and an egg yolk with a little milk to bind the mixture.

3 Divide the mixture into 6 or 8 and shape into thick or thin sausages.

4 Whisk the remaining egg white until frothy. Coat the sausages first in the egg white and then in the crisp breadcrumbs.

5 Heat the dripping and fry the sausages for 6 minutes until golden brown. Serve.

2

3

1

ricotta-stuffed chicken with tomato

Stuffed with creamy ricotta, spinach and garlic, then gently cooked in a rich tomato sauce, this is a suitable dish to make in advance.

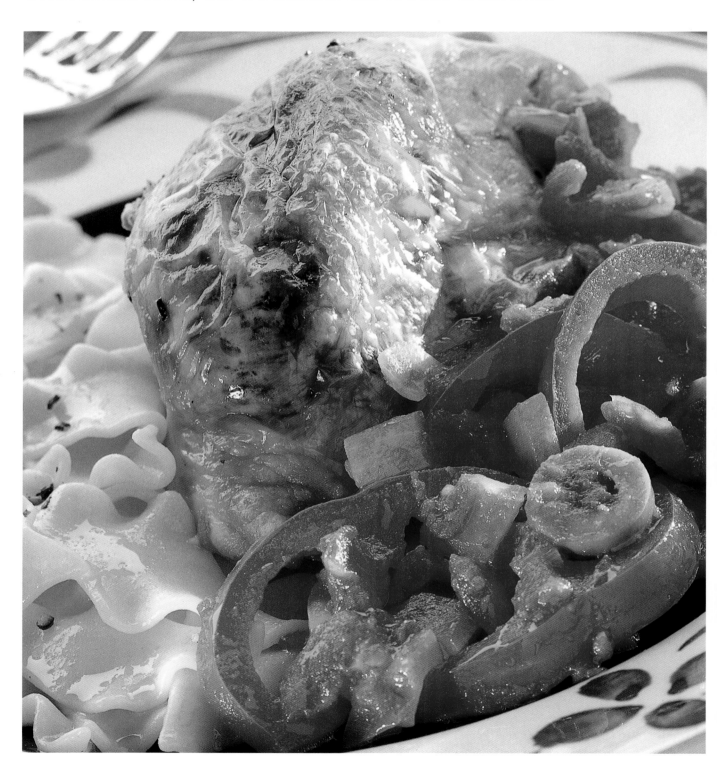

Serves 4

4 part-boned chicken breasts

125 g/4½ oz frozen spinach, defrosted

150 g/5½ oz ricotta cheese

2 garlic cloves, crushed

salt and pepper

1 tbsp olive oil

1 onion, chopped

1 red pepper, sliced

400 g/14 oz can chopped tomatoes

6 tbsp wine or chicken stock

10 stuffed olives, sliced

pasta, to serve

1 Make a slit between the skin and meat on one side of each chicken breast. Lift the skin to form a pocket, being careful to leave the skin attached to the other side.

2 Put the spinach into a sieve and press out the water with a spoon. Mix with the ricotta, half the garlic and seasoning.

3 Spoon the spinach mixture under the skin of each chicken breast then secure the edge of the skin with cocktail sticks.

4 Heat the oil in a frying pan, add the onion and fry for a minute, stirring. Add the remaining garlic and red pepper and cook for 2 minutes. Stir in the tomatoes, wine or stock, olives and seasoning. Set the sauce aside and chill the chicken if preparing in advance.

5 Bring the sauce to the boil, pour into a shallow ovenproof dish and arrange the chicken breasts on top in a single layer.

3

5

6 Cook, uncovered in a preheated oven, 200°C/400°F/Gas Mark 6, for 35 minutes until the chicken is golden and cooked through. Test by making a slit in one of the chicken breasts with a skewer to make sure the juices run clear and not pink. Spoon a little of the sauce over the chicken breasts then transfer to serving plates. Serve with pasta.

1

chicken toad-in-the-hole cakes

This unusual recipe uses chicken and Cumberland sausage, which is then made into individual bite-sized cakes.

2

3

5

Serves 4-6

125 g/4½ oz plain flour

pinch of salt

1 egg, beaten

200 ml/7 fl oz milk

75 ml/3 fl oz water

2 tbsp beef dripping

250 g/9 oz chicken breasts

250 g/9 oz Cumberland sausage

chicken or onion gravy, to serve (opional)

1 Mix the flour and salt in a bowl, make a well in the centre and add the beaten egg.

2 Add half the milk, and using a wooden spoon, work in the flour slowly.

3 Beat the mixture until smooth, then add the remaining milk and water.

4 Beat again until the mixture is smooth. Let the mixture stand for at least 1 hour.

5 Add the dripping to individual baking tins or to one large baking tin. Cut up the chicken and sausage so that you get a generous piece in each individual tin or several scattered around the large tin.

6 Heat in a preheated oven, 220°C/425°F/Gas Mark 7, for 5 minutes until very hot. Remove the tins from the oven and pour in the batter, leaving space for the mixture to expand.

7 Return to the oven to cook for 35 minutes, until risen and golden brown. Do not open the oven door for at least 30 minutes.

8 Serve hot, with chicken or onion gravy, or alone.

variation

Use skinless, boneless chicken legs instead of chicken breast in the recipe. Cut up as directed. Use your favourite variety of sausage instead of Cumberland sausage.

chicken pieces with two dips

Very simple to make and easy to eat with fingers, this dish can be served warm for a light lunch or cold as part of a buffet.

Serves 2

2 boneless chicken breasts

15 g/½ oz plain flour

1 tbsp sunflower oil

PEANUT DIP

3 tbsp smooth or crunchy peanut butter

4 tbsp natural yogurt

1 tsp grated orange rind

orange juice (optional)

TOMATO DIP

1 medium tomato

5 tbsp creamy fromage frais

2 tsp tomato purée

1 tsp chopped fresh chives

1 Using a sharp knife, slice the chicken into fairly thin strips and toss in the flour to coat.

2 Heat the oil in a non-stick pan and fry the chicken until golden and thoroughly cooked. Remove the chicken strips from the pan and drain well on kitchen paper.

3 To make the peanut dip, mix together all the ingredients in a bowl. If liked, add a little orange juice to thin the consistency.

4 To make the tomato dip, chop the tomato and mix with the remaining ingredients.

5 Serve the chicken strips with the dips and a selection of vegetable sticks for dipping.

cook's tip

For a lower-fat alternative, poach the strips of chicken in a small amount of boiling chicken stock for 6-8 minutes.

variation

For a refreshing guacamole dip, combine 1 mashed avocado, 2 finely chopped spring onions, 1 chopped tomato, 1 crushed garlic clove and a squeeze of lemon juice. Remember to add the lemon juice immediately after the avocado has been mashed to prevent discoloration.

1

2

4

chicken & wine risotto with saffron

This famous dish is known throughout the world, and it is perhaps the best known of all Italian risottos, although there are many variations.

Serves 4

125 g/4½ oz butter

900 g/2 lb chicken meat, sliced thinly

1 large onion, chopped

500 g/1 lb 2 oz arborio rice

600 ml/1 pint chicken stock

150 ml/½ pint white wine

1 tsp crumbled saffron

salt and pepper

60 g/2 oz grated Parmesan cheese, to serve

1 Heat 60 g/2 oz of the butter in a deep frying pan, and fry the chicken and onion until golden brown.

2 Add the rice, stir well, and cook for 15 minutes.

3 Heat the stock until boiling and gradually add to the rice. Add the white wine, saffron, salt and pepper to taste and mix well. Simmer gently for 20 minutes, stirring occasionally, and adding more stock if the risotto becomes too dry.

4 Leave to stand for a few minutes and just before serving add a little more stock and simmer for a further 10 minutes. Serve the risotto, sprinkled with the grated Parmesan cheese and the remaining butter.

1

3

2

cook's tip

A risotto should have moist but separate grains. Stock should be added a little at a time and only when the last addition has been completely absorbed.

variation

The possibilities for risotto are endless — try adding the following just at the end of cooking time: cashew nuts and sweetcorn, lightly sautéed courgettes and basil, or artichokes and oyster mushrooms.

chicken cottage pie

This recipe is a type of cottage pie and is just as versatile. Add vegetables and herbs of your choice, depending on what you have at hand.

Serves 4

500 g/1 lb 2 oz minced chicken

1 large onion, chopped finely

2 carrots, diced finely

25 g/1 oz plain flour

1 tbsp tomato purée

300 ml/1½ pint chicken stock

salt and pepper

pinch of fresh thyme

900 g/2 lb potatoes, creamed with butter
    and milk and highly seasoned

90 g/3 oz grated Lancashire cheese

peas, to serve

variation

Instead of Lancashire cheese, you could sprinkle Cotswold cheese over the top. This is a tasty blend of Double Gloucester, onion and chives, and is ideal for melting as a topping. Alternatively, you could use a mixture of cheeses, depending on whatever you have at hand.

3

4

5

1 Dry-fry the minced chicken, onion and carrots in a non-stick saucepan for 5 minutes, stirring frequently.

2 Sprinkle the chicken with the flour and simmer for a further 2 minutes.

3 Gradually blend in the tomato purée and stock then simmer for 15 minutes. Season and add the thyme.

4 Transfer the chicken and vegetable mixture to an ovenproof casserole and allow to cool.

5 Spoon the mashed potato over the chicken mixture and sprinkle with the Lancashire cheese. Bake in a preheated oven, 200°C/400°F/Gas Mark 6, for 20 minutes, or until the cheese is bubbling and golden, then serve with the peas.

baked chicken & mozzarella

This method of cooking makes the chicken aromatic and succulent. It also reduces the amount of oil needed since the chicken and vegetables cook in their own juices.

Serves 6

1 tbsp olive oil

6 skinless chicken breast fillets

250 g/9 oz mozzarella cheese

500 g/1 lb 2 oz courgettes, sliced

6 large tomatoes, sliced

pepper

1 small bunch fresh basil or oregano

rice or pasta, to serve

2

3

4

1 Cut six pieces of foil each about 25cm/10 inches square. Brush the foil squares lightly with oil and set aside until required.

2 With a sharp knife, slash each chicken breast at intervals, then slice the mozzarella cheese and place between the cuts in the chicken.

3 Divide the courgettes and tomatoes between the pieces of foil and sprinkle with black pepper. Tear or roughly chop the basil or oregano and scatter over the vegetables in each parcel.

4 Place the chicken on top of each pile of vegetables then wrap in the foil to enclose the chicken and vegetables, tucking in the ends.

5 Place on a baking tray and bake in a preheated oven, 200°C/400°F/Gas Mark 6, for about 30 minutes.

6 To serve, unwrap each foil parcel and serve with rice or pasta.

cook's tip

To aid cooking, place the vegetables and chicken on the shiny side of the foil so that once the parcel is wrapped up the dull surface of the foil is facing outwards. This ensures that the heat is absorbed into the parcel and not reflected away from it.

italian risotto

If you prefer, ordinary long grain rice can be used instead of arborio rice, but it won't give you the traditional, deliciously creamy texture that is typical of Italian risottos.

Serves 4

2 tbsp sunflower oil

15 g/½ oz butter or margarine

1 medium leek, thinly sliced

1 large yellow pepper, diced

3 skinless, boneless chicken breasts, diced

350 g/12 oz arborio rice

few strands saffron

salt and pepper

1.5 litres/2¾ pints chicken stock

200 g/7 oz can sweetcorn

60 g/2 oz toasted unsalted peanuts

60 g/2 oz grated Parmesan cheese

1

2

1 Heat the oil and butter or margarine in a large saucepan. Fry the leek and pepper for 1 minute then stir in the chicken and cook, stirring until golden brown.

2 Stir in the rice and cook for 2–3 minutes.

3 Stir in the saffron strands, and salt and pepper to taste. Add the stock, a little at a time, cover and cook over a low heat, stirring occasionally, for about 20 minutes, until the rice is tender and most of the liquid is absorbed. Do not let the risotto dry out – add more stock if necessary.

4 Stir in the sweetcorn, peanuts and Parmesan cheese, then adjust the seasoning to taste. Serve hot.

4

cook's tip

Risottos can be frozen, before adding the Parmesan cheese, for up to 1 month, but remember to reheat this risotto thoroughly as it contains chicken.

chicken & grapes with cream sauce

Chicken is surprisingly delicious when combined with fruits such as grapes or gooseberries.

Serves 4

15 g/½ oz butter

1 tbsp sunflower oil

4 skinless, boneless chicken breasts

4 shallots, finely chopped

150 ml/½ pint chicken stock

1 tbsp cider vinegar

175 g/6 oz halved seedless grapes

120 ml/4 fl oz double cream

1 tsp freshly grated nutmeg

salt and pepper

cornflour, to thicken (optional)

variation

If desired, add a little dry white wine or vermouth to the sauce in step 3.

1 Heat the butter and sunflower oil in a wide, flameproof casserole or pan and quickly fry the chicken breasts until golden brown, turning once. Remove the chicken breasts and keep warm while you are cooking the shallots.

2 Add the chopped shallots to the pan and fry gently until softened and lightly browned. Return the chicken breasts to the pan.

3 Add the chicken stock and cider vinegar to the pan, bring to the boil then cover and simmer gently for 10–12 minutes, stirring occasionally.

3

1

4

4 Transfer the chicken to a serving dish. Add the grapes, cream and nutmeg to the pan. Heat through, seasoning with salt and pepper to taste. Add a little cornflour to thicken the sauce, if desired. Pour the sauce over the chicken and serve.

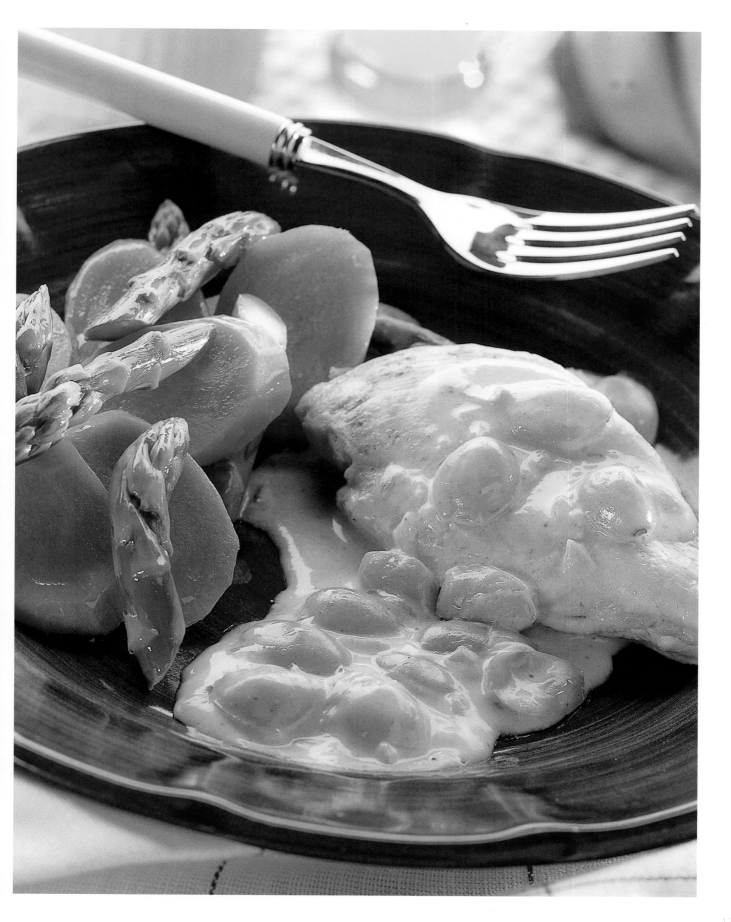

flambéed chicken

If you prefer, just use boneless chicken breasts in this recipe. This dish has a surprising combination of coffee and brandy flavours.

1

Serves 4

4 chicken breasts or suprêmes,
   each about 125 g/4½ oz

4 tbsp corn oil

8 shallots, sliced

rind and juice of 1 lemon

2 tsp Worcestershire sauce

4 tbsp chicken stock

1 tbsp chopped fresh parsley

3 tbsp coffee liqueur

3 tbsp brandy, warmed

2

3

1 Place the chicken breasts or suprêmes on a chopping board, cover with clingfilm and pound them until flattened with a wooden meat mallet or a rolling pin.

2 Heat the oil in a large frying pan and fry the chicken for 3 minutes on each side. Add the shallots and cook for a further 3 minutes.

3 Sprinkle with lemon juice and lemon rind and add the Worcestershire sauce and chicken stock. Cook for 2 minutes, then sprinkle with the chopped fresh parsley.

4 Add the coffee liqueur and the brandy and flame the chicken by lighting the spirit with a taper or long match. Cook until the flame is extinguished, then serve.

cook's tip

A suprême is a chicken fillet that sometimes has part of the wing bone remaining. Chicken breasts can be used instead.

honeyed orange chicken

A glossy glaze with sweet and fruity flavours coats chicken breasts in this tasty recipe. The minty rice makes the dish complete.

Serves 6

6 boneless chicken breasts

1 tsp turmeric

1 tbsp wholegrain mustard

300 ml/½ pint orange juice

2 tbsp clear honey

2 tbsp sunflower oil

350 g/12 oz long grain rice

1 orange

3 tbsp chopped mint

salt and pepper

mint sprigs, to garnish

1

1 With a sharp knife, mark the surface of the chicken breasts in a diamond pattern. Mix together the turmeric, mustard, orange juice and honey and pour over the chicken. Chill until required.

2 Lift the chicken from the marinade and pat dry on kitchen paper.

3 Heat the oil in a wide pan, add the chicken and sauté until golden, turning once. Drain off any excess oil. Pour over the marinade, cover and simmer for 10–15 minutes until the chicken is tender.

2

5

4 Boil the rice in lightly salted water until tender and drain well. Finely grate the rind from the orange and stir into the rice with the mint.

5 Using a sharp knife, remove the peel and white pith from the orange and cut the flesh into segments.

6 Serve the chicken with the orange and mint rice, garnished with orange segments and mint sprigs.

variation

To make a slightly sharper sauce, use small grapefruit instead of the oranges.

chicken morsels with parsley & vegetables

This colourful, simple dish will tempt the appetites of all the family — it is ideal for toddlers, who enjoy the fun shapes of the multi-coloured peppers.

Serves 4

10 skinless, boneless chicken thighs

1 medium onion

1 each medium red, green and yellow peppers

1 tbsp sunflower oil

400 g/14 oz can chopped tomatoes

2 tbsp chopped fresh parsley

pepper

wholemeal bread and a green salad, to serve

1 Using a sharp knife, cut the chicken thighs into bite-sized pieces.

2 Peel and thinly slice the onion. Halve and deseed the peppers and cut into small diamond shapes.

4

1

2

3 Heat the oil in a shallow frying pan. Add the chicken and onion and fry quickly until golden.

4 Add the peppers, cook for 2–3 minutes, then stir in the tomatoes and parsley and season with pepper.

5 Cover tightly and simmer for about 15 minutes, until the chicken and vegetables are tender. Serve hot with wholemeal bread and a green salad.

cook's tip

You can use dried parsley instead of fresh but remember that you only need about one half of dried to fresh.

cook's tip

If you are making this dish for small children, the chicken can be finely chopped or minced first.

chicken fusilli

Steaming allows you to cook without fat, and these little foil parcels
retain all the natural juices of the chicken while cooking conveniently
over the pasta while it boils.

2

3

6

Serves 4

4 skinless, boneless, chicken breasts

25 g/1 oz fresh basil leaves

15 g/½ oz hazelnuts

1 garlic clove, crushed

salt and pepper

250 g/9 oz wholemeal pasta spirals

2 sun-dried tomatoes or fresh tomatoes

1 tbsp lemon juice

1 tbsp olive oil

1 tbsp capers

60 g/2 oz black olives

cook's tip

Sun-dried tomatoes have a wonderful, rich flavour, but if you can't find them use fresh tomatoes.

1 Beat the chicken breasts with a rolling pin to flatten evenly.

2 Place the basil and hazelnuts in a food processor and process until finely chopped. Mix with the garlic, salt and pepper.

3 Spread the basil mixture over the chicken breasts and roll up from one short end to enclose the filling. Wrap the chicken roll tightly in foil so that they hold their shape, then seal the ends well.

4 Bring a large pan of lightly salted water to the boil and cook the pasta until tender, but still firm to the bite.

5 Place the chicken parcels in a steamer basket or colander set over the pan, cover tightly, and steam for 10 minutes. Meanwhile, dice the tomatoes.

6 Drain the pasta and return to the pan with the lemon juice, olive oil, tomatoes, capers and olives. Heat through.

7 Pierce the chicken with a skewer to make sure that the juices run clear and not pink, then slice the chicken, arrange over the pasta and serve.

creamy paprika chicken

This subtly spiced chicken is spiked with cayenne pepper and paprika and finished off with a fruity sauce.

Serves 2-3

25 g/1 oz plain flour

1 tbsp cayenne pepper

1 tsp paprika

350 g/12 oz skinless, boneless chicken, diced

25 g/1 oz butter

1 onion, chopped finely

450 ml/16 fl oz milk, warmed

4 tbsp apple purée

125 g/4½ oz green grapes

150 ml/¼ pint soured cream

sprinkle of paprika

1 Mix the flour, cayenne pepper and paprika together and use to coat the chicken.

2 Shake off any excess flour. Melt the butter in a saucepan and gently fry the chicken with the onion for 4 minutes.

3 Stir in the flour and spice mixture. Add the milk slowly, stirring until the sauce thickens.

4 Simmer until the sauce is smooth.

5 Add the apple purée and grapes and simmer gently for 20 minutes.

6 Transfer the chicken and devilled sauce to a serving dish and top with soured cream and a sprinkle of paprika.

variation

For a healthier alternative to soured cream, use natural yogurt.

cook's tip

Add more paprika if desired — as it is quite a mild spice, you can add plenty without it being too overpowering.

1

3

5

chicken parcels with lemon grass

A healthy recipe with a delicate oriental flavour, ideal for tender young summer vegetables. You'll need large spinach leaves to wrap around the chicken, but make sure they are young leaves.

1

Serves 4

4 boneless, skinless chicken breasts

1 tsp ground lemon grass

salt and pepper

2 spring onions, chopped finely

250 g/9 oz young carrots

250 g/9 oz young courgettes

2 sticks celery

1 tsp light soy sauce

250 g/9 oz spinach leaves

2 tsp sesame oil

2

1 With a sharp knife, make a slit through one side of each chicken breast, to open out a large pocket. Sprinkle the inside of the pocket with lemon grass, salt and pepper. Tuck the spring onions into the pockets.

2 Trim the carrots, courgettes and celery then cut into small matchsticks. Plunge them into a pan of boiling water for 1 minute, drain and toss in the soy sauce.

3

3 Pack the vegetables into the pockets in each chicken breast and fold over firmly to enclose. Reserve any remaining vegetables. Wash the spinach leaves thoroughly, then drain and pat dry with paper towels. Wrap the chicken breasts firmly in the spinach leaves to enclose completely. If the leaves are too firm to wrap the chicken easily, steam them for a few seconds until they are softened and flexible.

4 Place the wrapped chicken in a steamer and steam over rapidly boiling water for 20–25 minutes, depending on size.

5 Stir-fry any leftover vegetable sticks and spinach for 1–2 minutes in the sesame oil and serve with the chicken.

spinach-stuffed chicken with parma ham

Stuffed with creamy ricotta, nutmeg and spinach, then wrapped with wafer thin slices of Parma ham and gently cooked in white wine.

Serves 4

125 g/4½ oz frozen spinach, defrosted

125 g/4½ oz ricotta cheese

pinch grated nutmeg

salt and pepper

4 skinless, boneless chicken breasts, each weighing 175 g/6 oz

4 Parma ham slices

25 g/1 oz butter

1 tbsp olive oil

12 small onions or shallots

125 g/4½ oz button mushrooms, sliced

1 tbsp plain flour

150 ml/¼ pint dry white or red wine

300 ml/½ pint chicken stock

carrot purée and green beans, to serve (optional)

1 Put the spinach into a sieve and press out the water with a spoon. Mix with the ricotta and nutmeg and season with salt and pepper to taste.

2 Using a sharp knife, slit each chicken breast through the side and enlarge each cut to form a pocket. Fill with the spinach mixture, reshape the chicken breasts, wrap each breast tightly in a slice of ham and secure with cocktail sticks. Cover and chill in the refrigerator.

3 Heat the butter and oil in a frying pan and brown the chicken breasts for 2 minutes on each side. Transfer the chicken to a large, shallow ovenproof dish and keep warm until required.

4 Fry the onions (or shallots, if using) and mushrooms for 2–3 minutes until lightly browned. Stir in the plain flour then gradually add the wine and stock. Bring to the boil, stirring constantly. Season and spoon the mixture around the chicken.

5 Cook the chicken uncovered in a preheated oven, 200°C/400°F/Gas Mark 6, for 20 minutes. Turn the breasts over and cook for a further 10 minutes. Remove the cocktail sticks and serve with the sauce, together with carrot purée and green beans, if wished.

2

3

4

chicken breasts with red & yellow sauces

This quick and simple dish is colourful and healthy. It would be perfect for an impromptu lunch or supper dish.

Serves 4

2 tbsp olive oil

2 medium onions, chopped finely

2 garlic cloves, crushed

2 red peppers, chopped

good pinch cayenne pepper

2 tsp tomato purée

2 yellow peppers, chopped

pinch of dried basil

4 skinless, boneless chicken breasts

150 ml/¼ pint dry white wine

150 ml/¼ pint chicken stock

bouquet garni

salt and pepper

fresh herbs, to garnish

1 Heat 1 tablespoon of oil in each of two medium-sized saucepans. Place half the chopped onions, 1 of the garlic cloves, the red peppers, the cayenne pepper and the tomato purée in one of the saucepans. Place the remaining onion, garlic, yellow peppers and basil in the other pan.

2 Cover each pan and cook over a very low heat for 1 hour until the peppers are soft. If either mixture becomes dry, add a little water. Work each mixture separately in a food processor, then sieve separately.

3 Return the separate mixtures to the pans and season. The two sauces can be gently reheated while the chicken is cooking.

4 Put the chicken breasts into a frying pan and add the wine and stock. Add the bouquet garni and bring the liquid to simmer. Cook the chicken for about 20 minutes until tender.

5 To serve, pour a serving of each sauce on to four serving plates, slice the chicken breasts and arrange on the plates. Garnish with fresh herbs.

1

3

4

cook's tip

Make your own bouquet garni by tying together sprigs of your favourite herbs with string, or wrap up dried herbs in a piece of muslin. A popular combination is thyme, parsley and bay.

chicken slices with horseradish & honey

After cooking with stock and vegetables, chicken breasts are served with a velvety sauce made from whisky and crème fraîche.

Serves 6

25 g/1 oz butter

60 g/2 oz shredded leeks

60 g/2 oz diced carrot

60 g/2 oz diced celery

4 shallots, sliced

600 ml/1 pint chicken stock

6 chicken breasts

50 ml/2 fl oz whisky

200 ml/7 fl oz crème fraîche

2 tbsp freshly grated horseradish

1 tsp honey, warmed

1 tsp chopped fresh parsley

salt and pepper

sprig of fresh parsley, to garnish

1

5

3

1 Melt the butter in a large saucepan and add the leeks, carrot, celery and shallots. Cook for 3 minutes, add half the chicken stock and cook for about 8 minutes.

2 Add the remaining chicken stock, bring to the boil, add the chicken breasts and cook for 10 minutes.

3 Remove the chicken and thinly slice. Place on a large, hot serving dish and keep warm until required.

4 In another saucepan, heat the whisky until reduced by half. Strain the chicken stock through a fine sieve, add to the pan and reduce the liquid by half.

5 Add the crème fraîche, the horseradish and the honey. Heat gently and add the chopped parsley and salt and pepper to taste. Stir until well blended.

6 Pour a little of the whisky sauce around the chicken and pour the remaining sauce into a sauceboat to serve.

7 Serve with a vegetable patty made from the leftover vegetables, mashed potato and fresh vegetables. Garnish with the parsley sprig.

Long, slow cooking means meltingly succulent meat with a good, rich flavour. Because chicken itself does not have a strong flavour, it marries happily with almost any other ingredient, herb or spice. The recipes in this section are drawn from many cuisines from around the world, and there are dishes from Italy, France, Hungary, the Caribbean and the USA. French classics include Bourguignonne of Chicken and Brittany Chicken Casserole.

The aroma of roasting chicken is always tempting and this section includes the traditional roast chicken, with all the trimmings, as well as many other imaginative treatments. Unusual stuffings to try are courgette and lime, marmalade, or oat and herb stuffing. Many of the recipes in this section exploit the complementary flavours of chicken and fruits and there are some enticing taste combinations.

casseroles, stews& roasts

roast chicken & mushroom casserole

This unusual chicken dish has the flavour of roast chicken but is finished off in a casserole with a wild mushroom sauce.

Serves 4

90 g/3 oz butter, softened

1 garlic clove, crushed

salt and pepper

1 large chicken

175 g/6 oz wild mushrooms

12 shallots

25 g/1 oz plain flour

150 ml/¼ pint brandy

300 ml/½ pint double cream

1 tbsp chopped fresh parsley, to garnish

wild rice or roast potatoes, and green beans,
   to serve

2

1 Place the butter, garlic, and salt and pepper in a bowl and combine well.

2 Rub the mixture inside and outside of the chicken and leave for 2 hours.

3 Place the chicken in a large roasting tin and roast in the centre of a preheated oven, 230°C/450°F/Gas Mark 8, for 1½ hours, basting with the garlic butter every ten minutes.

4 Remove the chicken from the roasting tin and set aside to cool slightly.

5 Transfer the chicken juices to a saucepan and cook the mushrooms and shallots for 5 minutes. Sprinkle with the flour. Add the warm brandy and ignite using a taper or long match.

6 Add the double cream and cook for 3 minutes on a very low heat, stirring all the time.

5

6

7 Remove the bones and cut the chicken into small bite-sized pieces, then place the meat in a casserole dish. Cover with the mushroom sauce and bake in the oven, with the heat reduced to 160°C/325°F/Gas Mark 3, for a further 12 minutes. Garnish with the parsley and serve with wild rice or roast potatoes, and green beans.

chicken suprêmes with port & cherry sauce

This recipe is rather time-consuming but it is well worth the effort. Cherries and chicken make a good flavour combination.

Serves 6

6 large chicken suprêmes

6 black peppercorns, crushed

300 g/10½ oz pitted black cherries, or
    canned pitted cherries

12 shallots, sliced

4 slices rindless, streaky bacon, chopped

8 juniper berries

4 tbsp port

150 ml/¼ pint red wine

25 g/1 oz butter

2 tbsp walnut oil

25 g/1 oz flour

salt and pepper

new potatoes and green beans, to serve

1

4

1 Place the chicken in an ovenproof dish. Add the peppercorns, cherries or canned cherries, and their juice, if using, and the shallots.

2 Add the bacon, juniper berries, port and red wine. Season well.

3 Place the chicken in the refrigerator and leave to marinate for 48 hours.

4 Heat the butter and walnut oil in a large frying pan. Remove the chicken from the marinade and fry quickly in the pan for 4 minutes on each side.

5 Return the chicken to the marinade, reserving the butter, oil and juices in the pan.

6 Cover with foil and bake in a preheated oven, 180°C/350°F/ Gas Mark 4, for 20 minutes. Transfer the chicken from the baking tin to a warm serving dish. Add the flour to the juices in the frying pan and cook for 4 minutes, add the marinade and bring to the boil then simmer for 10 minutes until the sauce reaches a smooth consistency.

7 Pour the cherry sauce over the chicken suprêmes and serve with new potatoes and green beans.

5

chicken in wine with herbs & mushrooms

Napoleon's chef was ordered to cook a sumptuous meal on the eve of the battle of Marengo. He gathered everything possible to make a feast, and this was the result.

Serves 4

1 tbsp olive oil

8 chicken pieces

300 g/10½ oz passata

200 ml/7 fl oz white wine

2 tsp dried mixed herbs

40 g/1½ oz butter, melted

2 garlic cloves, crushed

8 slices white bread

100 g/3½ oz mixed mushrooms (such as
   button, oyster and ceps)

40 g/1¾ oz black olives, chopped

1 tsp sugar

fresh basil, to garnish

1 Using a sharp knife, remove the bone from each of the chicken pieces.

2 Heat the oil in a large frying pan. Add the chicken pieces and cook for 4–5 minutes, turning occassionally, or until browned all over.

3 Add the passata, wine and mixed herbs to the frying pan. Bring to the boil and then leave to simmer for 30 minutes or until the chicken is tender and the juices run clear when a skewer is inserted into the thickest part of the meat.

4 Make bruschetta. Mix the melted butter and crushed garlic together. Lightly toast the slices of bread and brush with the garlic butter.

5 Add the remaining oil to a separate frying pan and cook the mushrooms for 2–3 minutes or until just brown.

6 Add the olives and sugar to the chicken mixture and warm through.

7 Transfer the chicken and sauce to serving plates. Serve with the bruschetta and fried mushrooms.

cook's tip

If you have time, marinate the chicken pieces in the wine and herbs and leave in the refrigerator for 2 hours. This will make the chicken more tender and accentuate the wine flavour of the sauce.

braised chicken & vegetables with dumplings

Root vegetables are always cheap and nutritious, and combined with chicken they make tasty and economical casseroles.

Serves 4

4 chicken quarters

2 tbsp sunflower oil

2 medium leeks

250 g/9 oz carrots, chopped

250 g/9 oz parsnips, chopped

2 small turnips, chopped

600 ml/1 pint chicken stock

3 tbsp Worcestershire sauce

2 sprigs fresh rosemary

salt and pepper

DUMPLINGS

200 g/7 oz self-raising flour

100 g/3½ oz shredded suet

1 tbsp chopped rosemary leaves

cold water, to mix

1 Remove the skin from the chicken if you prefer. Heat the oil in a large, flameproof casserole or heavy saucepan and fry the chicken until golden. Using a slotted spoon, remove the chicken from the pan. Drain off the excess fat.

2 Trim and slice the leeks. Add the carrots, parsnips and turnips to the casserole and cook for 5 minutes, until lightly coloured. Return the chicken to the pan.

3 Add the chicken stock, Worcestershire sauce, rosemary and seasoning, then bring to the boil.

4 Reduce the heat, cover and simmer gently for about 50 minutes or until the juices run clear when the chicken is pierced with a skewer.

5 To make the dumplings, combine the flour, suet and rosemary leaves with salt and pepper in a bowl. Stir in just enough cold water to bind to a firm dough.

6 Form into 8 small balls and place on top of the chicken and vegetables. Cover and simmer for a further 10–12 minutes, until the dumplings are well risen. Serve with the casserole.

chicken, bean & beetroot casserole

A hearty, one-dish meal that would make a substantial lunch or supper. As it requires a long cooking time, make double quantities and freeze half to eat later.

Serves 6

500 g/1 lb 2 oz beans, such as flageolets, soaked overnight and drained

25 g/1 oz butter

2 tbsp olive oil

3 rindless bacon slices, chopped

900 g/1¾ lb chicken pieces

1 tbsp plain flour

300 ml/½ pint cider

150 ml/¼ pint chicken stock

salt and pepper

14 shallots

2 tbsp honey, warmed

250 g/8 oz ready-cooked beetroot

1 Cook the chosen beans in salted boiling water for about 25 minutes.

2 Heat the butter and olive oil in a flameproof casserole, add the bacon and chicken and cook for 5 minutes.

3 Sprinkle with the flour then add the cider and chicken stock, stirring constantly to prevent lumps forming. Season with salt and pepper to taste and bring to the boil.

4 Add the beans then cover the casserole tightly with a lid or cooking foil and bake in the centre of a preheated oven, 160°C/325°F/ Gas Mark 3, for 2 hours.

5 About 15 minutes before the end of cooking time, remove the lid or cooking foil from the casserole.

6 In a frying pan, gently cook the shallots and honey together for 5 minutes, turning the shallots frequently.

7 Add the shallots and cooked beetroot to the casserole and leave to finish cooking in the oven for the last 15 minutes.

cook's tip

To save time, use canned flageolet beans instead of dried. Drain and rinse before adding to the chicken.

3

4

6

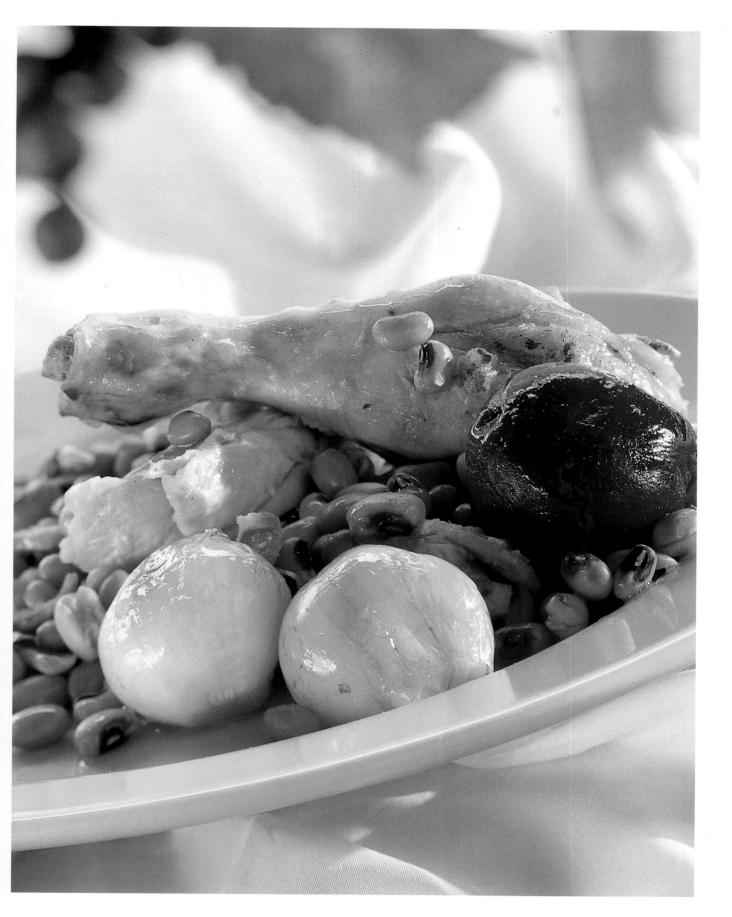

oriental chicken & ginger sauce

This recipe has an oriental flavour, which can be further enhanced with chopped spring onions, cinnamon and lemon grass.

Serves 6-8

6 tbsp sesame oil

900 g/1¾ lb chicken meat

60 g/2 oz flour, seasoned

32 shallots, sliced

500 g/1 lb 2 oz wild mushrooms,
   roughly chopped

300 ml/½ pint chicken stock

2 tbsp Worcestershire sauce

1 tbsp honey

2 tbsp grated fresh root ginger

salt and pepper

150 ml/¼ pint yogurt

flat leaf parsley, to garnish

wild rice and white rice, to serve

cook's tip

Mushrooms can be stored in the refrigerator for 24-36 hours. Keep them in paper bags as they 'sweat' in plastic. You do not need to peel mushrooms but wild mushrooms must be washed thoroughly.

1 Heat the oil in a large frying pan. Coat the chicken in the seasoned flour and cook for about 4 minutes, until browned all over. Transfer to a large deep casserole and keep warm until required.

2 Slowly fry the shallots and mushrooms in the juices.

3 Add the chicken stock, Worcestershire sauce, honey and fresh ginger, then season to taste with salt and pepper.

2

4

4 Pour the mixture over the chicken, and cover the casserole with a lid or cooking foil.

5 Cook in the centre of a preheated oven, 150°C/300°F/Gas Mark 2, for about 1½ hours, until the meat is very tender. Add the yogurt and cook for a further 10 minutes. Serve the casserole with a mixture of wild rice and white rice, and garnish with fresh parsley.

1

chicken, almond & grape casserole

Spices, herbs, fruit, nuts and vegetables are combined to make an appealing casserole with lots of flavour.

Serves 4-6

3 tbsp olive oil

900 g/2 lb chicken meat, sliced

10 shallots or pickling onions

3 carrots, chopped

60 g/2 oz chestnuts, sliced

60 g/2 oz flaked almonds, toasted

1 tsp freshly grated nutmeg

3 tsp ground cinnamon

300 ml/½ pint white wine

300 ml/½ pint chicken stock

175 ml/6 fl oz white wine vinegar

1 tbsp chopped fresh tarragon

1 tbsp chopped fresh flat leaf parsley

1 tbsp chopped fresh thyme

grated rind of 1 orange

1 tbsp dark muscovado sugar

sea salt and pepper

125 g/4½ oz seedless black grapes, halved

fresh herbs, to garnish

wild rice or puréed potato, to serve

1

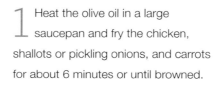

2

1 Heat the olive oil in a large saucepan and fry the chicken, shallots or pickling onions, and carrots for about 6 minutes or until browned.

2 Add the remaining ingredients, except the grapes, and simmer over a low heat for 2 hours until the meat is very tender. Stir the casserole occasionally.

3

3 Add the grapes just before serving. Garnish with herbs and serve with wild rice or puréed potato.

variation

Experiment with different types of nuts and fruits — try sunflower seeds instead of the almonds, and add 2 fresh apricots, chopped.

cook's tip

This casserole would also be delicious served with thick slices of crusty wholemeal bread to soak up the sauce.

chicken & green pea casserole

Pork fat adds a tasty flavour to this dish. If you can't find
fresh garden peas, frozen peas are a good substitute.

Serves 4

250 g/9 oz pork fat, cut into small cubes

60 g/2 oz butter

16 small onions or shallots

1 kg/2 lb 4 oz boneless chicken pieces

25 g/1 oz plain flour

600 ml/1 pint chicken stock

bouquet garni

500 g/1 lb 2 oz fresh peas

salt and pepper

1 Bring a saucepan of salted water to the boil and simmer the pork fat cubes for three minutes. Drain and dry the pork on absorbent paper towels.

2 Melt the butter in a large frying pan, add the pork and onions, fry gently for 3 minutes until lightly browned.

2

4

6

3 Remove the pork and onions from the pan and set aside until required. Add the chicken pieces to the pan and cook until browned all over. Transfer the chicken to an ovenproof casserole.

4 Add the flour to the pan and cook, stirring until it begins to brown, then slowly blend in the chicken stock.

5 Cook the chicken, with the sauce and bouquet garni, in a preheated oven, 200°C/400°F/Gas Mark 6, for 35 minutes.

6 Remove the bouquet garni about 10 minutes before the end of cooking time and add the peas and the reserved pork and onions. Stir to mix. Season to taste.

7 When cooked, place the chicken pieces on to a large platter, surrounded with the pork, peas and onions.

cook's tip

If you want to cut down on fat, use small cubes of lean bacon, rather than pork fat.

chicken & ham with sage & mixed rice

Cooking in a single pot means that all of the flavours are retained. This is a substantial meal that needs only a salad and some crusty bread.

Serves 4

1 large onion, chopped

1 garlic clove, crushed

2 sticks celery, sliced

2 carrots, diced

2 sprigs fresh sage

300 ml/½ pint chicken stock

350 g/12 oz boneless, skinless
   chicken breasts

225 g/8 oz mixed brown and wild rice

400 g/14 oz can chopped tomatoes

dash of Tabasco sauce

salt and pepper

2 medium courgettes, trimmed and
   thinly sliced

100 g/3½ oz lean ham, diced

fresh sage, to garnish

salad leaves and crusty bread, to serve

2

1 Place the onion, garlic, celery, carrots and sprigs of fresh sage in a large saucepan and pour in the chicken stock. Bring to the boil, cover the pan and simmer for 5 minutes.

2 Cut the chicken into 2.5 cm/1 inch cubes and stir into the pan with the vegetables. Cover the pan and continue to cook for a further 5 minutes.

3 Stir in the rice and chopped tomatoes. Add a dash of Tabasco sauce to taste and season well. Bring to the boil, cover and simmer for 25 minutes.

4 Stir in the sliced courgettes and diced ham and continue to cook, uncovered, for a further 10 minutes, stirring occasionally, until the rice is just tender.

5 Remove and discard the sprigs of sage. Garnish with a few sage leaves and serve with a fresh salad and crusty bread.

3

4

cook's tip

If you do not have fresh sage, use 1 tsp of dried sage in step 1.

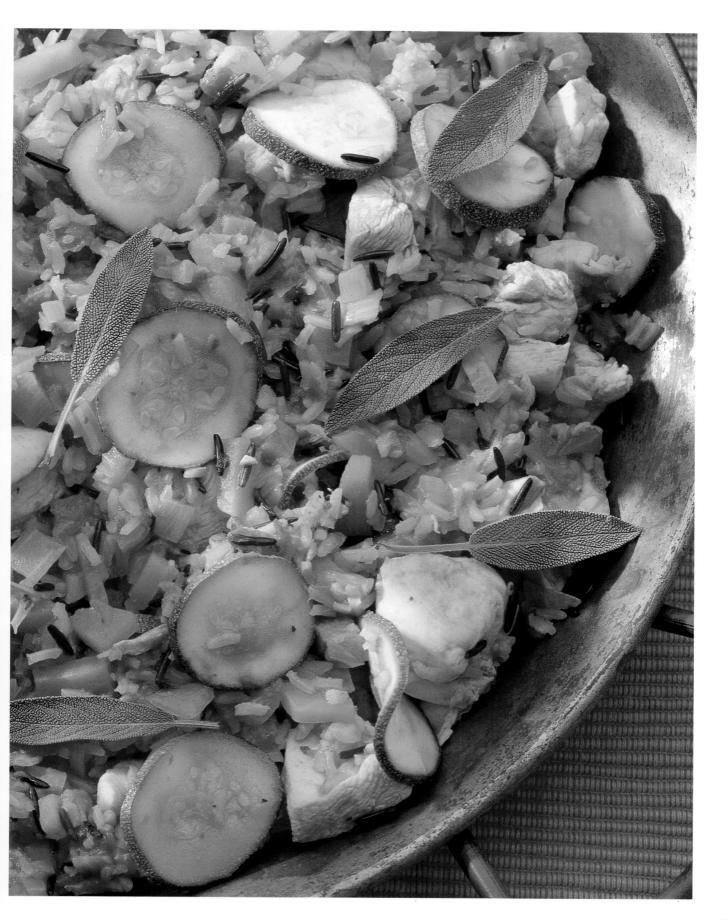

chicken & cannellini bean casserole

Low in fat and high in fibre, this colourful casserole makes a healthy and hearty meal for a cold winters day.

Serves 4

8 chicken drumsticks, skinned

1 tbsp wholemeal flour

1 tbsp olive oil

2 medium red onions

1 garlic clove, crushed

1 tsp fennel seeds

1 bay leaf

finely grated rind and juiceof 1 small orange

400 g/14 oz can chopped tomatoes

400 g/14 oz can cannellini or flageolet
    beans, drained

salt and pepper

3 thick slices wholemeal bread

2 tsp olive oil

2

3

5

1 Toss the chicken drumsticks in the flour to coat evenly. Heat the oil in a non-stick or heavy saucepan and fry the chicken over a fairly high heat, turning frquently, until golden brown. Transfer to a large ovenproof casserole and keep warm until required.

2 Slice the red onions into thin wedges. Add to the pan and cook for a few minutes until lightly browned. Stir in the garlic.

3 Add the fennel seeds, bay leaf, orange rind and juice, tomatoes, beans and seasoning.

4 Cover tightly and cook in a preheated oven, 190°C/375°F/ Gas Mark 5, for 30–35 minutes until the chicken juices are clear and not pink when pierced through the thickest part with a metal skewer.

5 For the topping, cut the bread into small dice and toss in the oil. Remove the lid from the casserole and top with the bread cubes. Bake for a further 15–20 minutes until the bread is golden and crisp. Serve hot.

cook's tip

Choose beans which are canned in water with no added sugar or salt. Drain and rinse well before use.

sherried chicken, bacon & plums

Full of the flavours of autumn, this combination of lean chicken, shallots, garlic and fresh, juicy plums is a very fruity blend. Serve with bread to mop up the gravy.

Serves 4

2 rashers lean back bacon, rinds removed, trimmed and chopped

1 tbsp sunflower oil

450 g/1 lb skinless, boneless chicken thighs, cut into 4 equal strips

1 garlic clove, crushed

175 g/6 oz shallots, halved

225 g/8 oz plums, halved or quartered (if large) and stoned

1 tbsp light muscovado sugar

150 ml/5 fl oz dry sherry

2 tbsp plum sauce

450 ml/16 fl oz fresh chicken stock

2 tsp cornflour mixed with 4 tsp cold water

2 tbsp fresh parsley, chopped, to garnish

crusty bread, to serve

1

2

2 In the same frying pan, heat the oil and fry the chicken with the garlic and shallots for 4–5 minutes, stirring occasionally, until well browned all over.

3 Return the bacon to the pan and stir in the plums, sugar, sherry, plum sauce and stock. Bring to the boil and simmer for 20 minutes until the plums have softened and the chicken is cooked through.

4 Add the cornflour mixture to the pan and cook, stirring, for a further 2–3 minutes until thickened.

5 Spoon the casserole on to warm serving plates and garnish with chopped parsley. Serve with chunks of crusty bread to mop up the fruity gravy.

1 In a large, non-stick frying pan, dry fry the bacon for 2–3 minutes until the juices run out. Remove the bacon from the pan with a slotted spoon, set aside and keep warm.

variation

Chunks of lean turkey or pork would also go well with this combination of flavours. The cooking time will remain the same.

3

casserole chicken with olives & thyme

A colourful casserole packed with sunshine flavours from the Mediterranean. Sun-dried tomatoes add a wonderful richness and you need very few to make this really special dish.

Serves 4

8 chicken thighs

2 tbsp olive oil

1 medium red onion, sliced

2 garlic cloves, crushed

1 large red pepper, sliced thickly

thinly pared rind and juice of 1 small orange

125 ml/4 floz chicken stock

400 g/14 oz can chopped tomatoes

25 g/1 oz sun-dried tomatoes, thinly sliced

1 tbsp chopped fresh thyme

50 g/1¾ oz pitted black olives

salt and pepper

thyme sprigs and orange rind, to garnish

crusty fresh bread, to serve

cook's tip

Sun-dried tomatoes have a dense texture and concentrated taste, and add intense flavour to slow-cooking casseroles.

1

2

1 In a heavy or non-stick large frying pan, fry the chicken without fat over a fairly high heat, turning occasionally until golden brown. Using a slotted spoon, drain off any excess fat from the chicken and transfer to a flameproof casserole.

2 Fry the onion, garlic and pepper in the pan over a moderate heat for 3–4 minutes. Transfer to the casserole.

3 Add the orange rind and juice, chicken stock, canned tomatoes and sun-dried tomatoes and stir to combine.

4 Bring to the boil then cover the casserole with a lid and simmer very gently over a low heat for about 1 hour, stirring occasionally. Add the chopped fresh thyme and pitted black olives, then adjust the seasoning with salt and pepper.

5 Scatter orange rind and thyme over the casserole to garnish, and serve with crusty bread.

3

chicken cassoulet

This is a cassoulet with a twist — it is made with chicken instead of duck and lamb. Save time by using canned beans, such as borlotti or cannellini beans, which are both good in this dish.

3

5

Serves 4

4 tbsp sunflower oil

900 g/1¾ lb chicken meat, chopped

250 g/9 oz mushrooms, sliced

16 shallots

6 garlic cloves, crushed

1 tbsp plain flour

250 ml/9 fl oz white wine

250 ml/9 fl oz chicken stock

1 bouquet garni (1 bay leaf, sprig thyme,
    celery, parsley & sage tied together
    with string)

salt and pepper

400 g/14 oz can borlotti beans

small squash, to serve

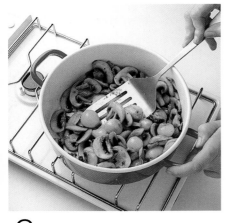

2

4 Add the white wine and chicken stock, stir until boiling, then add the bouquet garni. Season well with salt and pepper.

5 Drain the borlotti beans and rinse thoroughly, then add to the casserole.

6 Cover and place in the centre of a preheated oven, 150°C/ 300°F/ Gas Mark 2, for 2 hours. Remove the bouquet garni and serve the casserole with small squash.

1 Heat the sunflower oil in an ovenproof casserole and fry the chicken until browned all over. Remove the chicken from the casserole with a slotted spoon and set aside until required.

2 Add the mushrooms, shallots and garlic to the fat in the casserole and cook for 4 minutes.

3 Return the chicken to the casserole and sprinkle with the flour, then cook for a further 2 minutes.

cook's tip

Mushrooms are ideal in a low-fat diet because they are high in flavour and contain no fat. Experiment with the wealth of varieties that are now available from supermarkets.

cook's tip

Serve the casserole with brown rice to make this filling dish go even further.

chicken bourguignonne with melting hearts

A recipe based on a classic French dish. Use a good quality wine when making this casserole.

Serves 4-6

4 tbsp sunflower oil

900 g/1¾ lb chicken meat, diced

250 g/9 oz button mushrooms

125 g/4½ oz rindless, smoked bacon, diced

16 shallots

2 garlic cloves, crushed

1 tbsp plain flour

150 ml/¼ pint white Burgundy wine

150 ml/¼ pint chicken stock

1 bouquet garni (1 bay leaf, sprig thyme,
    stick of celery, parsley and sage tied
    with string)

salt and pepper

deep-fried croûtons and a selection of
    cooked vegetables, to serve

cook's tip

A good quality red wine can be used instead of the white wine, to produce a rich, glossy red sauce.

1

3

2

3 Return the chicken to the casserole and sprinkle with flour. Cook for a further 2 minutes, stirring.

4 Add the Burgundy wine and chicken stock to the casserole and stir until boiling. Add the bouquet garni and season well with salt and pepper.

5 Cover the casserole and bake in the centre of a preheated oven, 150°C/300°F/Gas Mark 2, for 1½ hours. Remove the bouquet garni.

6 Deep fry some heart-shaped croûtons (about 8 large ones) in beef dripping and serve with the bourguignonne.

1 Heat the sunflower oil in an ovenproof casserole and brown the chicken all over. Remove from the casserole with a slotted spoon.

2 Add the mushrooms, bacon, shallots and garlic to the casserole and cook for 4 minutes.

chicken goulash with claret & cream

Goulash is traditionally made with beef, but this recipe successfully uses chicken instead. To reduce fat, use a low-fat cream in place of the soured cream.

Serves 6

900 g/1¾ lb chicken meat, diced

60 g/2 oz flour, seasoned with 1 tsp paprika,
    salt and pepper

2 tbsp olive oil

25 g/1 oz butter

1 onion, sliced

24 shallots, peeled

1 each red and green pepper, chopped

1 tbsp paprika

1 tsp rosemary, crushed

4 tbsp tomato purée

300 ml/½ pint chicken stock

150 ml/¼ pint claret

400 g/14 oz can chopped tomatoes

150 ml/¼ pint soured cream

1 tbsp chopped fresh parsley, to garnish

chunks of bread and a side salad, to serve

2

3

1 Toss the chicken in the seasoned flour until it is coated all over.

2 In a flameproof casserole, heat the oil and butter and fry the onion, shallots and peppers for 3 minutes.

3 Add the chicken and cook for a further 4 minutes.

4 Sprinkle with the paprika and rosemary.

4

5 Add the tomato purée, chicken stock, claret and chopped tomatoes, cover and cook in the centre of a preheated oven, 160°C/325°F/ Gas Mark 3 for 1½ hours.

6 Remove the casserole from the oven, allow it to stand for 4 minutes, then add the soured cream and garnish with parsley.

7 Serve with chunks of bread and a side salad.

variation

Serve the goulash with buttered ribbon noodles instead of bread. For an authentic touch, try a Hungarian red wine instead of the claret.

traditional chicken stew

This is a slow-cooked, old-fashioned stew to warm up a wintery day. The rarebit toasts are a perfect accompaniment to soak up the rich juices, but if you prefer, serve the stew with jacket potatoes.

Serves 4-6

4 large, skinless chicken thighs

2 tbsp plain flour

2 tbsp English mustard powder

2 tbsp sunflower oil

15 g/½ oz butter

4 small onions

600 ml/1 pint beer

2 tbsp Worcestershire sauce

3 tbsp chopped fresh sage leaves

salt and pepper

RAREBIT TOASTS

60 g/2 oz grated mature English Cheddar

1 tsp English mustard powder

1 tsp plain flour

1 tsp Worcestershire sauce

1 tbsp beer

2 slices wholemeal toast

green vegetable and new potatoes to serve

1

3

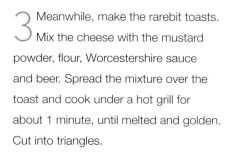

2

1 Trim any excess fat from the chicken and toss in the flour and mustard powder to coat evenly. Heat the sunflower oil and butter in a large flameproof casserole and fry the chicken over a fairly high heat, turning occasionally, until golden. Remove the chicken from the casserole with a slotted spoon and keep hot.

2 Peel the onions and slice into wedges, then fry quickly until golden. Add the chicken, beer, Worcestershire sauce, fresh sage, and salt and pepper to taste. Bring to the boil, cover and simmer very gently for about 1½ hours, until the chicken is very tender.

3 Meanwhile, make the rarebit toasts. Mix the cheese with the mustard powder, flour, Worcestershire sauce and beer. Spread the mixture over the toast and cook under a hot grill for about 1 minute, until melted and golden. Cut into triangles.

4 Stir the sage leaves into the chicken stew, bring to the boil and serve with the rarebit toasts, a green vegetable and new potatoes.

cook's tip

If you do not have fresh sage, use 2 tsp of dried sage in step 2.

chicken & lime stew

The addition of lime juice and lime rind adds a delicious tangy flavour to this chicken stew while the peppers add a splash of colour.

Serves 4

1 large chicken, cut into small portions

60 g/2 oz flour, seasoned

2 tbsp oil

500 g/1 lb 2 oz baby onions or shallots, sliced

1 each green and red pepper, sliced thinly

150 ml/¼ pint chicken stock

juice and rind of 2 limes

2 chillies, chopped

2 tbsp oyster sauce

1 tsp Worcestershire sauce

salt and pepper

1 Coat the chicken pieces in the seasoned flour. Heat the oil in a large frying pan and cook the chicken for about 4 minutes until browned all over.

2 Using a slotted spoon, transfer the chicken to a large, deep casserole and sprinkle with the sliced onions. Keep warm until required.

3 Slowly fry the peppers in the juices remaining in the frying pan.

4 Add the chicken stock, lime juice and rind and cook for a further 5 minutes.

5 Add the chillies, oyster sauce and Worcestershire sauce. Season with salt and pepper to taste.

6 Pour the peppers and juices over the chicken and onions.

7 Cover the casserole with a lid or cooking foil.

8 Cook in the centre of a preheated oven, 190°C/375°F/Gas Mark 5, for 1½ hours until the chicken is very tender, then serve.

cook's tip

Try this casserole with a cheese scone topping. About 30 minutes before the end of cooking time, simply top with rounds cut from cheese scone pastry.

2

4

6

caribbean chicken hotpot

A tasty way to make chicken joints go a long way, this hearty casserole, spiced with the warm, subtle flavour of ginger, is a good choice for a Halloween party.

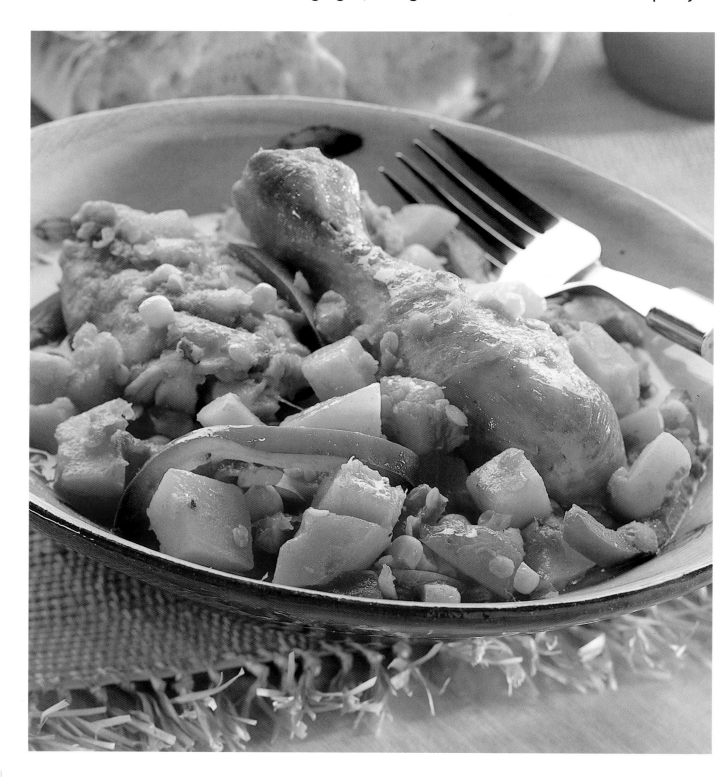

Serves 4

2 tsp sunflower oil

4 chicken drumsticks

4 chicken thighs

1 medium onion

750 g/1 lb 10 oz piece squash
  or pumpkin, diced

1 green pepper, sliced

2.5 cm/1 inch fresh ginger root, chopped
  finely

400 g/14 oz can chopped tomatoes

300 ml/½ pint chicken stock

60 g/2 oz split lentils

garlic salt

cayenne pepper

350 g/12 oz can sweetcorn

crusty bread, to serve

2

2

2

4 Cover the casserole and place in a preheated oven, 190°C/375°F/ Gas Mark 5, for about 1 hour, until the vegetables are tender and the chicken juices run clear when pierced with a skewer.

5 Add the drained sweetcorn and cook for a further 5 minutes. Season to taste and serve with crusty bread.

1 Heat the oil in a large flameproof casserole and fry the chicken joints until golden, turning frequently.

2 Using a sharp knife, peel and slice the onion, peel and dice the pumpkin or squash and deseed and slice the pepper.

3 Drain any excess fat from the pan and add the prepared onion, pumpkin and pepper. Gently fry for a few minutes until lightly browned. Add the chopped ginger, tomatoes, chicken stock and lentils. Season lightly with garlic salt and cayenne pepper.

variation

If you can't find fresh ginger root, add 1 tsp allspice for a warm, fragrant aroma.

variation

If squash or pumpkin is not available, swede makes a good substitute.

chicken & herb hotpot

There are many regional versions of hot-pot, all using fresh, local ingredients. Now, there are an endless variety of ingredients available all year, perfect for traditional one-pot cooking.

Serves 4

4 chicken quarters

6 medium potatoes, cut into
   5 mm/¼ inch slices

salt and pepper

2 sprigs thyme

2 sprigs rosemary

2 bay leaves

200 g/7 oz rindless, smoked streaky
   bacon, diced

1 large onion, chopped finely

200 g/7 oz sliced carrots

150 ml/¼ pint stout

25 g/1 oz melted butter

2

4

3

1 Remove the skin from the chicken
   quarters, if preferred.

2 Arrange a layer of potato slices in
   the bottom of a wide casserole.
Season with salt and pepper, then add
the thyme, rosemary and bay leaves.

3 Top with the chicken quarters, then
   sprinkle with the diced bacon,
onion and carrots. Season well and
arrange the remaining potato slices on
top, overlapping slightly.

4 Pour over the stout, brush the
   potatoes with the melted butter
and cover with a lid.

5 Bake in a preheated oven,
   150°C/300°F/Gas Mark 2, for
about 2 hours, uncovering for the last 30
minutes to allow the potatoes to brown.
Serve hot.

cook's tip

Serve the hotpot with
dumplings for a truly
hearty meal.

variation

This dish is also delicious
with stewing lamb, cut into
chunks. You can add different
vegetables depending on what
is in season — try leeks and
swedes for a slightly sweeter
flavour.

chicken bacon casserole with madeira wine

Madeira is a fortified wine which can be used in both sweet and savoury dishes. Here it adds a rich, full flavour to the casserole.

Serves 8

25 g/1 oz butter

20 baby onions

250 g/9 oz carrots, sliced

250 g/9 oz bacon, chopped

250 g/9 oz button mushrooms

1 chicken, weighing about 1.5 kg/3 lb 5 oz

425 ml/15 fl oz white wine

25 g/1 oz seasoned flour

425ml/15 fl oz chicken stock

salt and pepper

bouquet garni

150 ml/¼ pint Madeira wine

mashed potato or pasta, to serve

cook's tip

You can add any combination of herbs to this recipe — chervil is a popular herb in French cuisine, but add it at the end of cooking so that its delicate flavour is not lost. Other herbs which work well with chicken are parsley and tarragon.

1 Heat the butter in a large frying pan and fry the onions, carrots, bacon and button mushrooms for 3 minutes, stirring frequently. Transfer to a large casserole dish.

2 Add the chicken to the frying pan and brown all over. Transfer to the casserole dish with the vegetables and bacon.

2

3

4

3 Add the white wine and cook until the wine is nearly completely reduced.

4 Sprinkle with the seasoned flour, stirring to avoid lumps from forming.

5 Add the chicken stock, salt and pepper to taste and the bouquet garni. Cover and cook the casserole for 2 hours. About 30 minutes before the end of cooking time, add the Madeira wine and continue cooking uncovered.

6 Carve the chicken and serve with mashed potato or pasta.

baked chicken in batter with corn fritters

It is better if you have time to bone the chicken completely, or use chicken breast after removing all the fat and skin.

Serves 4-6

175 g/6 oz plain flour

1 tsp paprika

1 tsp freeze-dried Italian seasoning

1 tsp freeze-dried tarragon

1 tsp rosemary, finely crushed

2 eggs, beaten

120 ml/4 fl oz milk

1 chicken, weighing about 2 kg/4 lb, jointed

seasoned flour

150 ml/¼ pint rapeseed oil

2 bananas, quartered

1 apple, cut into rings,

350 g/12 oz can sweetcorn and peppers,
    drained

oil for frying

bunch of watercress

peppercorn or horseradish sauce, to serve

1 Mix together the flour, spices, herbs and a pinch of salt in a large bowl. Make a well in the centre and add the eggs.

2 Blend and slowly add the milk, whisking until very smooth.

3 Coat the chicken pieces with seasoned flour and dip the chicken pieces into the batter mix.

4 Heat the oil in a large frying pan. Add the chicken and fry for about 3 minutes or until lightly browned all over. Place the chicken pieces on a non-stick baking tray.

5 Batter the bananas and apple rings and fry for 2 minutes.

6 Finally toss the sweetcorn into the leftover batter.

7 Heat a little oil in a frying pan. Drop in spoonfuls of the sweetcorn mixture to make flat patty cakes. Cook for 4 minutes on each side. Keep warm with the apple and banana fritters.

8 Bake the chicken in a preheated oven, 200°C/400°F/Gas Mark 6, for about 25 minutes until the chicken is tender and golden brown.

9 Arrange the chicken, sweetcorn fritters, and the apple and banana fritters on a bed of fresh watercress. Serve with a peppercorn or horseradish sauce.

3

1

7

chicken, bean & celery bake

This economical bake is a complete meal — its crusty, herb-flavoured French bread topping mops up the tasty juices, and means there's no need to serve potatoes or rice separately.

Serves 4

2 tbsp sunflower oil

4 chicken quarters

16 small whole onions, peeled

3 sticks celery, sliced

400 g/14 oz can red kidney beans

4 medium tomatoes, quartered

200 ml/7 fl oz dry cider or stock

4 tbsp chopped fresh parsley

salt and pepper

1 tsp paprika

60 g/2 oz butter

12 slices French bread

2

2

1 Heat the oil in a flameproof casserole and fry the chicken quarters two at a time until golden. Using a slotted spoon, remove the chicken from the pan and set aside until required.

2 Add the onions and fry, turning occasionally, until golden brown. Add the celery and fry for 2–3 minutes. Return the chicken to the pan, then stir in the beans, tomatoes, cider, half the parsley, salt and pepper. Sprinkle with the paprika.

3 Cover and cook in a preheated oven, 200°C/400°F/Gas Mark 6, for 20–25 minutes, until the chicken juices run clear when pierced with a skewer.

4

4 Mix the remaining parsley with the butter and spread evenly over the French bread.

5 Uncover the casserole, arrange the bread slices overlapping on top and bake for a further 10–12 minutes, until golden and crisp.

cook's tip

Add a crushed garlic clove to the parsley butter for extra flavour.

variation

For a more unusual Italian tasting dish, replace the garlic and parsley bread topping with the pesto-covered toasts.

crispy baked chicken with cheese & mustard

Cheese and mustard, and a simple, crispy coating, make a delicious combination for this healthy dish.

Serves 4

1 tbsp milk

2 tbsp prepared English mustard

60 g/2 oz grated mature Cheddar cheese

3 tbsp plain flour

2 tbsp chopped fresh chives

4 skinless, boneless chicken breasts

jacket potatoes and fresh vegetables or
    crisp salad, to serve

1 Mix together the milk and mustard
  in a bowl. In another bowl, combine
the cheese, flour and chives.

2 Dip the chicken into the milk and
  mustard mixture, brushing to coat
evenly.

3 Dip the chicken breasts into the
  cheese mixture, pressing to coat
evenly. Place on a baking tray and
spoon any spare cheese coating over
the top.

1

2

4 Bake in a preheated oven,
  200°C/400°F/Gas Mark 6, for
30–35 minutes, or until golden brown
and the juices run clear, not pink, when
pierced with a skewer. Serve the
chicken hot, with jacket potatoes and
fresh vegetables, or serve cold, with
a crisp salad.

3

variation

There are several varieties
of mustard available. For a
sharper flavour try French
varieties — Meaux mustard has
a grainy texture with a warm,
spicy flavour while Dijon
mustard is medium-hot and
tangy.

cook's tip

It is a good idea to freeze
herbs as they retain their
colour, flavour and nutrients
very well. Chives are
particularly suitable for
freezing — store them in
labelled plastic bags and
shake them dry before use.
Dried chives are not an
adequate substitute for fresh.

feta chicken with mountain herbs

Chicken goes well with most savoury herbs, especially during the summer, when fresh herbs are at their best. This combination makes a good partner for tangy feta cheese and sun-ripened tomatoes.

Serves 4

8 skinless, boneless chicken thighs

2 tbsp each chopped fresh thyme, rosemary
and oregano

125 g/4½ oz feta cheese

1 tbsp milk

2 tbsp plain flour

thyme, rosemary and oregano, to garnish

TOMATO SAUCE

1 medium onion, roughly chopped

1 garlic clove, crushed

1 tbsp olive oil

4 medium plum tomatoes, quartered

sprig each of thyme, rosemary and oregano

salt and pepper

2

3

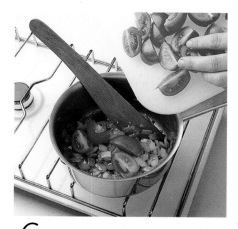

6

1 Spread out the chicken thighs on a
board, smooth side downwards.

2 Divide the herbs among the chicken
thighs, then cut the cheese into
eight sticks. Place one stick of cheese
in the centre of each chicken thigh.
Season well, then roll up to enclose
the cheese.

3 Place the rolls in an ovenproof dish,
brush with milk and dust with flour
to coat evenly.

4 Bake in a preheated oven,
190°C/375°F/Gas Mark 5, for
25–30 minutes, or until golden brown.
The juices should run clear and not pink
when the chicken is pierced with a
skewer in the thickest part.

5 To make the sauce, cook the onion
and garlic in the olive oil, stirring,
until softened and beginning to brown.

6 Add the tomatoes, reduce the heat,
cover and simmer gently for
15–20 minutes or until soft.

7 Add the herbs, then transfer to a
food processor and blend to a
purée. Press through a sieve to make a
smooth, rich sauce. Season to taste and
serve the sauce with the chicken,
garnished with herbs.

chicken with courgette & lime stuffing

A cheesy stuffing is tucked under the breast skin of the chicken to give added flavour and moistness to the meat.

Serves 6

340 g/12 oz courgettes

90 g/3 oz medium-fat soft cheese

finely grated rind of 1 lime

2 tbsp fresh breadcrumbs

salt and pepper

1 chicken, weighing 2.25 kg/5 lb

oil for brushing

25 g/1 oz butter

juice of 1 lime

cook's tip

For quicker cooking, finely grate the courgettes rather than cutting them into strips.

2

3

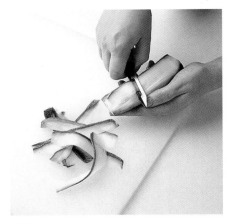

5

1 To make the stuffing, trim and coarsely grate 90 g/3 oz courgette and mix with the cheese, lime rind, breadcrumbs, salt and pepper.

2 Carefully ease the skin away from the breast of the chicken.

3 Push the stuffing under the skin with your fingers, to cover the breast evenly.

4 Place the chicken in a baking tin, brush with oil and roast in a preheated oven, 190°C/375°F/Gas Mark 5, for 20 minutes per 500 g/1 lb 2 oz plus 20 minutes, or until the juices run clear when the thickest part of the chicken is pierced with a skewer.

5 Meanwhile, trim the remaining courgettes and cut into long, thin strips with a potato peeler or sharp knife. Sauté in the butter and lime juice until just tender, then serve with the chicken.

spanish chicken with peaches & sherry

The Catalan region of Spain is famous for its wonderful combinations of meat with fruit. In this recipe, peaches lend a touch of sweetness and pine nuts, cinnamon and sherry add an unusual twist.

1

4

Serves 6

60 g/2 oz fresh brown breadcrumbs

60 g/2 oz pine nuts

1 small egg, beaten

4 tbsp chopped fresh thyme or
    1 tbsp dried thyme

4 fresh peaches or 8 canned peach halves

1 chicken, weighing about 2.5 kg/5½ lb

1 tsp ground cinnamon

200 ml/7 fl oz Amontillado sherry

4 tbsp double cream

salt and pepper

3

6 Sprinkle the remaining pine nuts over the remaining peach halves and place in an ovenproof dish in the oven for the final 10 minutes of cooking time.

7 Lift the chicken on to a serving plate and arrange the peach halves around it. Skim any fat from the juices, stir in the cream and heat gently. Serve with the chicken.

1 Combine the breadcrumbs with 25 g/1 oz pine nuts, the egg and the thyme.

2 Halve and stone the peaches, removing the skin if necessary. Dice one peach into small pieces and stir into the breadcrumb mixture. Season well. Spoon the stuffing into the neck cavity of the chicken, securing the skin firmly over it.

3 Place the chicken in a roasting tin. Sprinkle the cinnamon over the skin.

4 Cover loosely with foil and roast in a preheated oven, 190°C/375°F/Gas Mark 5, for 1 hour, basting occasionally.

5 Remove the foil and spoon the sherry over the chicken. Cook for a further 30 minutes, basting with the sherry, until the juices run clear when the chicken is pierced in the thickest part with a skewer.

cook's tip

Canned apricot halves in natural juice make an easy storecupboard alternative.

scottish roast chicken with oat stuffing

An unusual change from a plain roast, with a distinctly warming Scottish flavour and a delicious oatmeal stuffing.

Serves 6

1 medium onion, finely chopped

1 stick celery, sliced thinly

25 g/1 oz butter or 1 tbsp sunflower oil

1 tsp dried thyme

4 tbsp porridge oats

4 tbsp chicken stock

salt and pepper

1 chicken, weighing 2 kg/4 lb 8 oz

oil, for brushing

1 tbsp heather honey

2 tbsp Scotch whisky

2 tbsp plain flour

300 ml/½ pint chicken stock

a green vegetable and sautéed
    potatoes, to serve

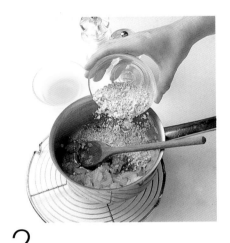

2

4

1 To make the stuffing, fry the onion and celery in the butter or oil, stirring over a moderate heat until softened and lightly browned.

2 Remove from the heat and stir in the thyme, oats, stock, salt and pepper.

3 Stuff the neck end of the chicken with the mixture and tuck the neck flap under. Place in a roasting tin, brush lightly with oil, and roast in a preheated oven, 190°C/375°F/Gas Mark 5, for about 1 hour.

4 Mix the heather honey with 1 tablespoon whisky and brush the mixture over the chicken. Return to the oven for a further 20 minutes, or until the chicken is golden brown and the juices run clear when the chicken is pierced through the thickest part with a skewer.

5 Lift the chicken on to a serving plate. Skim the fat from the juices then stir in the flour. Stir over a moderate heat until the mixture starts to bubble, then gradually add the stock and remaining whisky.

6 Bring to the boil, stirring, then simmer for 1 minute and serve the chicken with the sauce, a green vegetable and sautéed potatoes.

5

garlic chicken with mortadella

It's really very easy to bone a whole chicken, but if you prefer, you can ask a friendly butcher to do this for you.

Serves 6

1 chicken, weighing about 2.25 kg/5 lb

8 slices Mortadella or salami

125 g/4½ oz fresh white or brown
   breadcrumbs

125 g/4½ oz freshly grated
   Parmesan cheese

2 garlic cloves, crushed

6 tbsp chopped fresh basil or parsley

1 egg, beaten

pepper

olive oil

fresh spring vegetables, to serve

variation

Replace the Mortadella with
rashers of streaky bacon, if
preferred.

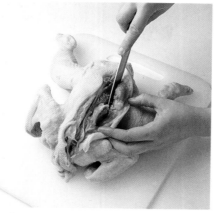

1

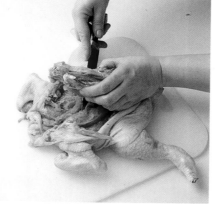

2

1 Bone the chicken, keeping the skin
   intact. Dislocate each leg by
breaking it at the thigh joint. Cut down
each side of the backbone, taking care
not to pierce the breast skin.

2 Pull the backbone clear of the flesh
   and discard. Remove the ribs,
severing any attached flesh with a sharp
knife.

3 Scrape the flesh from each leg and
   cut away the bone at the joint with
a knife or shears.

4 Use the bones for stock. Lay out
   the boned chicken on a board, skin
side down. Arrange the Mortadella slices
over the chicken, overlapping slightly.

5 Put the breadcrumbs, Parmesan,
   garlic and basil or parsley in a bowl.
Season well with pepper and mix. Stir in
the beaten egg to bind the mixture
together. Pile the mixture down the
middle of the boned chicken, roll the
meat around it and tie securely with fine
cotton string.

6 Place in a roasting dish and brush
   lightly with olive oil. Roast in a
preheated oven, 200°C/400°F/Gas
Mark 6, for 1½ hours or until the juices
run clear when pierced.

7 Serve hot or cold, in slices, with
   fresh spring vegetables.

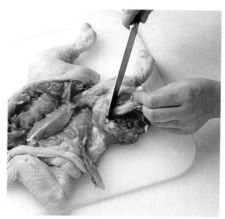

3

honeyed chicken with poppy seeds

Chicken portions are brushed with a classic combination of honey and mustard then a crunchy coating of poppy seeds is added.

1

Serves 4-6

8 chicken portions

60 g/2 oz butter, melted

4 tbsp mild mustard

4 tbsp clear honey

2 tbsp lemon juice

1 tsp paprika

salt and pepper

3 tbsp poppy seeds

tomato and sweetcorn salad, to serve

3

5

1 Place the chicken pieces, skinless side down, on a large baking tray.

2 Place all the ingredients except the poppy seeds into a large bowl and blend together thoroughly.

3 Brush the mixture over the chicken portions.

4 Bake in the centre of a preheated oven, 200°C/400°F/Gas Mark 6, for 15 minutes.

5 Carefully turn over the chicken pieces and coat the top side of the chicken with the remaining honey and mustard mixture.

6 Sprinkle the chicken with poppy seeds and return to the oven for a further 15 minutes.

7 Arrange the chicken on a serving dish, pour over the cooking juices and serve with a tomato and sweetcorn salad, if wished.

cook's tip

Mexican rice makes an excellent accompaniment to this dish: boil the rice for 10 minutes, drain, then fry for 5 minutes. Add chopped onions, garlic, tomatoes, carrots and chilli and cook for 1 minute before adding stock. Bring to the boil, cover and simmer for 20 minutes, adding more stock if necessary. Add peas 5 minutes before the end of the cooking time.

ham & sage chicken

Beetroot is one of the most underrated vegetables, adding flavour and colour to numerous dishes. Tender young beetroot are used in this recipe.

Serves 4

4 chicken suprêmes

8 fresh sage leaves

8 thin slices of York ham

250 g/9 oz Stilton cheese, cut into 8 slices

8 slices rindless streaky bacon

150 ml/1¼ pint chicken stock

2 tbsp port

24 shallots

500 g/1 lb 2 oz baby beetroot, cooked

1 tbsp cornflour, blended with a little port

salt and pepper

1 Cut a long slit horizontally along each chicken suprême to make a pocket.

2 Insert 2 sage leaves into each pocket and season lightly.

3 Wrap each slice of ham around a slice of cheese and place 2 into each chicken pocket. Carefully wrap enough bacon around each breast to completely cover the pockets containing the ham and the cheese.

4 Place the breasts in an ovenproof casserole dish and pour over the stock and port.

5 Add the shallots, cover with a lid or cooking foil and braise in a preheated oven, 190°C/375°F/Gas Mark 5, for about 40 minutes.

6 Carefully place each suprême on to a cutting board and slice through them to create a fan effect. Arrange on a warm serving dish with the shallots and beetroot.

7 Put the juices from the casserole into a saucepan and bring to the boil, remove from the heat and add the cornflour paste. Gently simmer and cook the sauce for 2 minutes, then pour over the shallots and beetroot before serving.

variation

Use any blue-veined cheese instead of the Stilton, if you prefer. Try Gorgonzola or Roquefort.

1

3

3

gardener's chicken

Any combination of small, young vegetables can be roasted with the chicken, such as courgettes, leeks and onions.

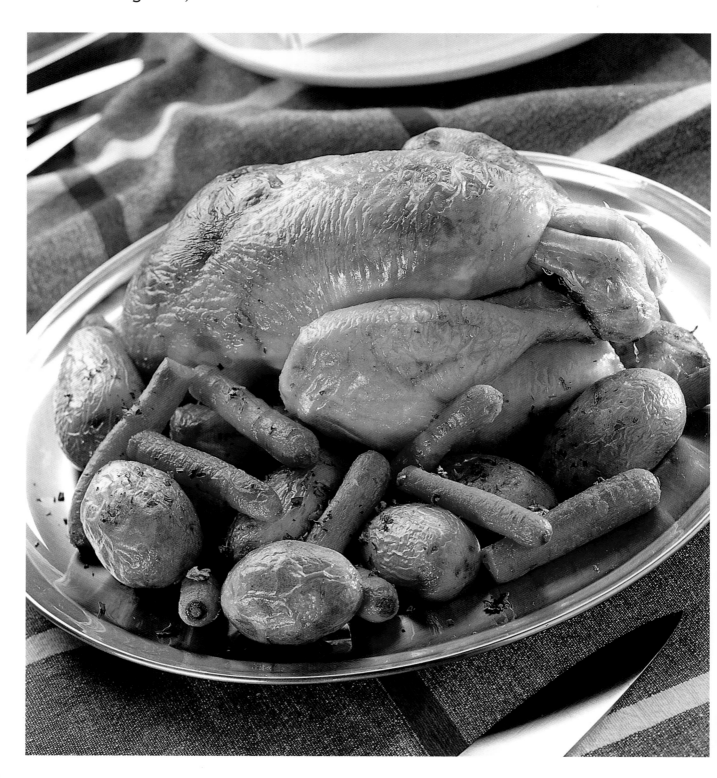

Serves 4

250 g/9 oz parsnips, peeled and chopped

125 g/4½ oz carrots, peeled and chopped

25 g/1 oz fresh breadcrumbs

¼ tsp grated nutmeg

1 tbsp chopped fresh parsley

salt and pepper

1.5 kg/3 lb 5 oz chicken

bunch parsley

½ onion

25 g/1 oz butter, softened

4 tbsp olive oil

500 g/1 lb 2 oz new potatoes, scrubbed

500 g/1 lb 2 oz baby carrots
washed and trimmed

chopped fresh parsley, to garnish

1 To make the stuffing, put the parsnips and carrots into a pan, half cover with water and bring to the boil. Cover the pan and simmer until tender. Drain well then purée in a blender or food processor. Transfer the purée to a bowl and leave to cool.

2 Mix in the breadcrumbs, nutmeg and parsley and season with salt and pepper.

3 Put the stuffing into the neck end of the chicken and push a little under the skin over the breast meat. Secure the flap of skin with a small metal skewer or cocktail stick.

4 Place the bunch of parsley and onion inside the cavity of the chicken, then place the chicken in a large roasting tin.

5 Spread the butter over the skin and season with salt and pepper, cover with foil and place in a preheated oven, 190°C/375°F/Gas Mark 5, for 30 minutes.

2

3

4

6 Meanwhile, heat the oil in a frying pan, and lightly brown the potatoes.

7 Transfer the potatoes to the roasting tin and add the baby carrots. Baste the chicken and continue to cook for a further hour, basting the chicken and vegetables after 30 minutes. Remove the foil for the last 20 minutes to allow the skin to crisp. Garnish the vegetables with chopped parsley and serve.

glazed cranberry chicken

This recipe, which uses a partly-boned chicken is easy to slice and serve. If you prefer, stuff in the traditional way at the neck end, and cook any remaining stuffing separately.

Serves 4

1 chicken, weighing about 2.25 kg/5 lb

1 ripe mango, diced

60g/2 oz fresh or frozen cranberries

125 g/4½ oz breadcrumbs

½ tsp ground mace

1 egg, beaten

salt and pepper

6 slices smoked bacon

½ tsp ground turmeric

2 tsp honey

2 tsp sunflower oil

1 To part-bone the chicken, dislocate the legs and place the chicken breast-side downwards. Cut a straight line through the skin along the ridge of the back. Scrape the meat down from the bone on both sides.

2 When you reach the point where the legs and wings join the body, cut through the joints. Work around the ribcage until the carcass can be lifted away.

3 Make six bacon rolls. For the stuffing, mix the mango with the cranberries, breadcrumbs and mace, then bind with egg. Season.

4 Place the chicken, skin-side down, and spoon over half the stuffing.

Arrange the bacon rolls down the centre then top with the remaining stuffing. Fold the skin over and tie with string. Turn the chicken over, truss the legs and tuck the wings underneath. Place in a roasting tin. Mix the turmeric, honey and oil and brush over the skin.

5 Roast in a preheated oven, 190°C/375°F/Gas Mark 5, for 1½–2 hours or until the juices run clear, not pink, when the chicken is pierced with a skewer. When the chicken starts to brown, cover loosely with foil to prevent overbrowning. Serve the chicken hot with seasonal vegetables.

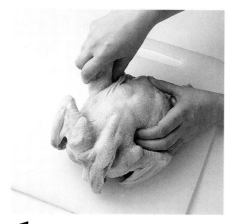

1

1

1

chicken & brandy pot roast

This colourful, nutritious pot roast could be served for a family meal or for a special dinner. Add more vegetables if you're feeding a crowd – if your roasting pot is large enough!

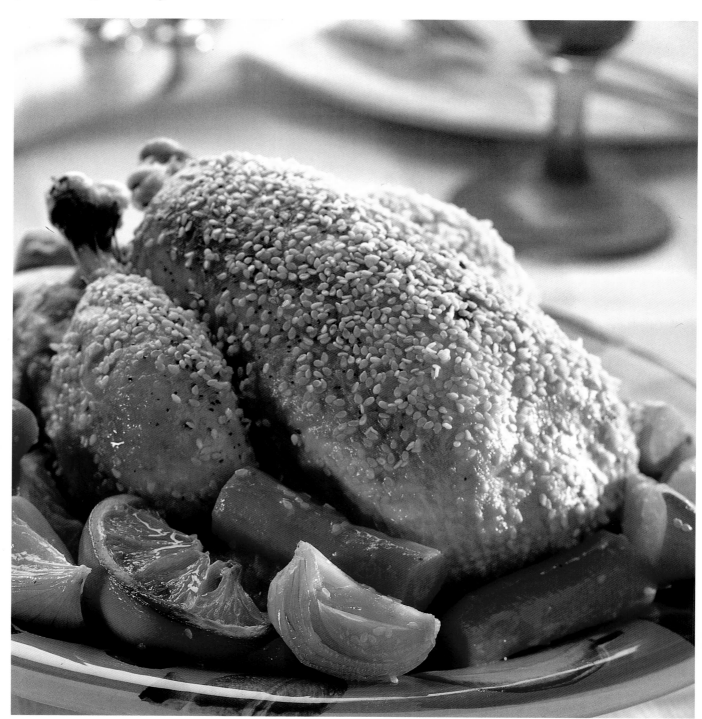

Serves 4

2 tbsp sunflower oil

1 chicken, weighing about 1.5 kg/3 lb 5 oz

2 large oranges

2 small onions, quartered

500 g/1 lb 2 oz small wholecarrots or thin
    carrots, cut into 5 cm/2 inch lengths

150 ml/¼ pint orange juice

2 tbsp brandy

2 tbsp sesame seeds

1 tbsp cornflour

salt and pepper

variation

Use lemons instead of oranges
for a sharper citrus flavour
and place a sprig of fresh
thyme in the chicken cavity
with the lemon half as they
are a good flavour
combination.

1 Heat the oil in a large flameproof casserole and fry the chicken, turning occasionally until evenly browned.

2 Cut one orange in half and place half inside the chicken cavity. Place the chicken in a large, deep casserole. Arrange the onions and carrots around the chicken.

2

3

4

3 Season well and pour over the orange juice.

4 Cut the remaining oranges into thin wedges and tuck around the chicken in the casserole, among the vegetables.

5 Cover and cook in a preheated oven, 180°C/350°F/Gas Mark 4, for about 1½ hours, or until there is no trace of pink in the chicken juices when pierced, and the vegetables are tender. Remove the lid and sprinkle with the brandy and sesame seeds, and return to the oven for 10 minutes.

6 To serve, lift the chicken on to a large platter. Place the vegetables around the chicken. Skim any excess fat from the juices. Blend the cornflour with 1 tablespoon cold water, then stir into the juices and bring to the boil, stirring all the time. Adjust the seasoning to taste, then serve the sauce with the chicken.

apple & redcurrant chicken with ham stuffing

The richly flavoured stuffing in this recipe is cooked under the breast skin of the chicken, so not only is all the flavour sealed in, but the chicken stays really moist and succulent during cooking.

Serves 6

15 g/½ oz butter

1 small onion, chopped finely

60 g/2 oz mushrooms, chopped finely

60 g/2 oz smoked ham, chopped finely

25 g/1 oz fresh breadcrumbs

1 tbsp chopped fresh parsley

3 crisp eating apples

1 tbsp lemon juice

1 chicken, weighing 2 kg/4 lb

oil, for brushing

15 g/½ oz butter

1 tbsp redcurrant jelly

mixed vegetables, to serve

salt and pepper

1 To make the stuffing, melt the butter and fry the onion gently, stirring until softened but not browned. Stir in the mushrooms and cook for 2–3 minutes. Remove from the heat and stir in the ham, breadcrumbs and the chopped parsley.

2 Core one of the apples, leaving the skin on, and grate coarsely. Add the stuffing mixture to the apple with the lemon juice. Season to taste.

3 Loosen the breast skin of the chicken and carefully spoon the stuffing mixture under it, smoothing the skin over evenly with your hands.

4 Place the chicken in a roasting tin and brush lightly with oil.

5 Roast the chicken in a preheated oven, 190°C/375°F/Gas Mark 5, for 25 minutes per 500 g/1 lb plus 25 minutes, or until there is no trace of pink in the juices when the chicken is pierced through the thickest part with a skewer. If the breast starts to brown too much, cover the chicken with foil.

6 Core and slice the remaining apples and sauté in the butter until golden. Stir in the redcurrant jelly and warm through until melted. Garnish the chicken with the apple slices and serve with mixed vegetables.

4

6

2

marmalade chicken with brandy sauce

Marmalade lovers will enjoy this festive recipe. You can use any favourite marmalade, such as lemon or grapefruit.

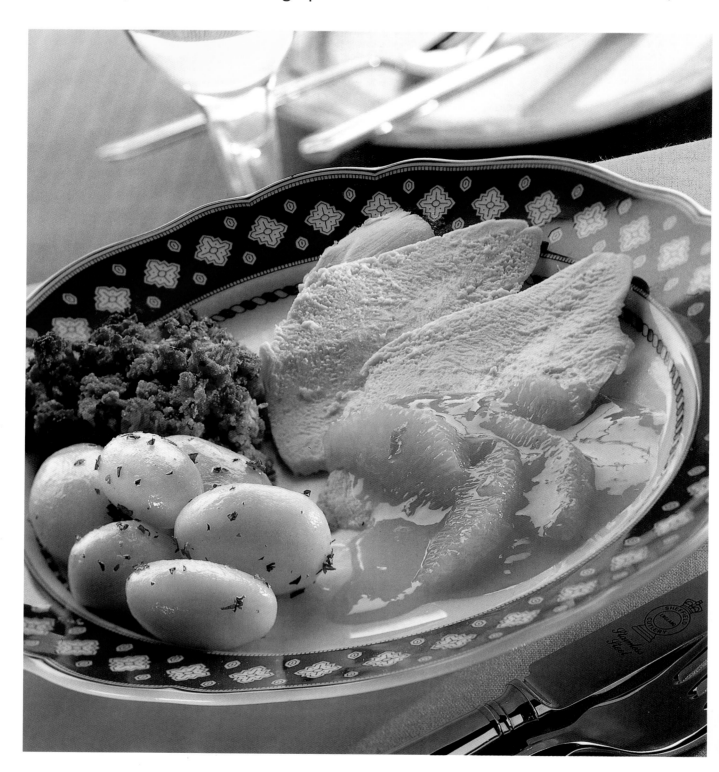

Serves 6

1 chicken, weighing about 2.25 kg/5 lb

bay leaves

STUFFING

1 stick celery, chopped finely

1 small onion, chopped finely

1 tbsp sunflower oil

125 g/4½ oz fresh wholemeal breadcrumbs

4 tbsp marmalade

2 tbsp chopped fresh parsley

1 egg, beaten

salt and pepper

SAUCE

2 tsp cornflour

2 tbsp orange juice

3 tbsp marmalade

150 ml/¼ pint chicken stock

1 medium orange

2 tbsp brandy

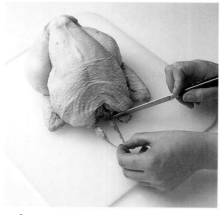

1

1

4

1 Lift the neck flap of the chicken and remove the wishbone using a small, sharp knife. Place a sprig of bay leaves inside the body cavity.

2 For the stuffing, sauté the celery and onion in the oil to soften. Add the breadcrumbs, 3 tablespoons of marmalade, parsley and egg. Season and use to stuff the neck cavity of the chicken. Any extra stuffing may be cooked separately.

3 Place the chicken in a roasting tin and brush lightly with oil. Roast in a preheated oven, 190°C/375°F/ Gas Mark 5 for 20 minutes per 500 g/ 1 lb 2 oz plus 20 minutes or until the juices run clear when the chicken is pierced in the thickest part with a skewer. Remove from the oven and glaze with the remaining marmalade.

4 Meanwhile, to make the sauce, blend the cornflour in a pan with the orange juice, then add the marmalade and chicken stock. Heat gently, stirring, until thickened and smooth. Remove from the heat. Cut the segments from the orange, discarding all white pith and membrane. Just before serving, add the orange segments and brandy to the sauce and bring to the boil.

5 Serve the chicken with the orange sauce, any extra stuffing and new potatoes.

mediterranean roast chicken

A roast that is full of Mediterranean flavour. A mixture of feta cheese, rosemary and sun-dried tomatoes is stuffed under the chicken skin, then roasted with garlic, new potatoes and vegetables.

Serves 6

2.5 kg/5 lb 8 oz chicken

sprigs of fresh rosemary

175 g/6 oz feta cheese, coarsely grated

2 tbsp sun-dried tomato paste

60 g/2 oz butter, softened

salt and pepper

1 bulb garlic

1 kg/2 lb 4 oz new potatoes, halved if large

1 each red, green and yellow pepper,
    cut into chunks

3 courgettes, sliced thinly

2 tbsp olive oil

2 tbsp plain flour

600 ml/1 pint chicken stock

2

4

3

1 Rinse the chicken inside and out with cold water and drain well. Carefully cut between the skin and the top of the breast meat using a small pointed knife. Slide a finger into the slit and carefully enlarge it to form a pocket. Continue until the skin is completely lifted away from both breasts and the top of the legs.

2 Chop the leaves from 3 rosemary sprigs. Mix with the feta, sun-dried tomato paste, butter and pepper then spoon under the skin. Put the chicken in a large roasting tin, cover with foil and cook in a preheated oven, 190°C/375°F/Gas Mark 5, for 20 minutes per 500 g/1 lb 2 oz plus 20 minutes.

3 Break the garlic bulb into cloves but do not peel. Add the vegetables to the chicken after 40 minutes.

4 Drizzle with oil, tuck in a few sprigs of rosemary and season well. Cook for the remaining time, removing the foil for the last 40 minutes to brown the chicken.

5 Transfer the chicken to a serving platter. Place some of the vegetables around the chicken and transfer the remainder to a warmed serving dish. Pour the fat out of the roasting tin and stir the flour into the remaining pan juices. Cook for 2 minutes then gradually stir in the stock. Bring to the boil, stirring until thickened. Strain into a sauce boat and serve with the chicken.

marinated chicken with tarragon

This fat-free recipe is great for summer entertaining served simply with a green salad and new potatoes. If you cut the chicken in half and press it flat, you can roast it in under an hour.

Serves 4

2 kg/4 lb 8 oz chicken

salt and pepper

MARINADE

300 ml/½ pint orange juice

3 tbsp cider vinegar

3 tbsp clear honey

2 tbsp chopped fresh tarragon

2 oranges, cut into wedges

SAUCE

handful of tarragon sprigs, chopped

200 g/7 oz fat-free fromage frais

2 tbsp orange juice

1 tsp clear honey

60 g/2 oz stuffed olives, chopped

tarragon sprigs, to garnish

1

2

1 Put the chicken on a chopping board with the breast downwards. Cut through the bottom part of the carcass using poultry shears or heavy kitchen scissors, making sure not to cut right through to the breast bone below.

2 Rinse the chicken with cold water, drain and place on a board with the skin side uppermost. Press the chicken flat, then cut off the leg ends.

3 Thread two long wooden skewers through the bird to keep it flat. Season the skin.

4 Put all the marinade ingredients, except the orange wedges, in a shallow, non-metallic dish. Mix, then add the chicken. Cover and chill for 4 hours, turning the chicken several times.

5 To make the sauce, mix all the ingredients and season. Spoon into a serving dish, cover and chill.

6 Transfer the chicken and marinade to a roasting tin, open out the chicken and place skin-side downwards. Tuck the orange wedges around the chicken and roast in a preheated oven, 200°C/400°F/Gas Mark 6, for 25 minutes. Turn the chicken over and roast for another 20–30 minutes. Baste until the chicken is browned and the juices run clear when pierced with a skewer. Garnish with tarragon and serve with the sauce.

3

bacon-wrapped chicken with redcurrants

Chicken suprêmes have a little bit of the wing bone remaining which makes them easy to pick up and eat. In this recipe, a tart, fruity sauce perfectly complements the chicken and dripping triangles.

Serves 8

60 g/2 oz butter

juice of 1 lemon

250 g/9 oz redcurrants or cranberries

1–2 tbsp muscovado sugar

salt and pepper

8 chicken suprêmes or breasts

16 slices of streaky bacon

thyme

60 g/2 oz beef dripping

4 slices of bread, cut into triangles

cook's tip

You can use either chopped fresh thyme or dried thyme in this recipe, but remember that dried herbs have a stronger flavour so you only need half the quantity compared to fresh herbs.

1

2

4

1 Heat the butter in a saucepan, add the lemon juice, redcurrants or cranberries, muscovado sugar and salt and pepper to taste. Cook for 1 minute and allow to cool until required.

2 Meanwhile, season the chicken with salt and pepper. Wrap 2 slices of streaky bacon around each breast and sprinkle with thyme.

3 Wrap each breast in a piece of lightly greased foil and place in a roasting tin. Roast in a preheated oven, 200°C/400°F/Gas Mark 6, for 15 minutes. Remove the foil and roast for another 10 minutes.

4 Heat the dripping in a frying pan, add the bread triangles and fry on both sides until golden brown.

5 Arrange the triangles on a large serving plate and top each with a chicken breast. Serve with a spoonful of the fruit sauce.

coriander chicken

This recipe for chicken is coated with a fresh-flavoured marinade then roasted. Try serving it with rice, yogurt and salad.

Serves 4-6

3 sprigs fresh coriander, chopped

4 garlic cloves

½ tsp salt

1 tsp pepper

4 tbsp lemon juice

4 tbsp olive oil

1 large chicken

sprig of fresh parsley, to garnish

boiled potatoes and carrots, to serve

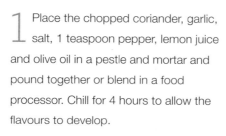

1 Place the chopped coriander, garlic, salt, 1 teaspoon pepper, lemon juice and olive oil in a pestle and mortar and pound together or blend in a food processor. Chill for 4 hours to allow the flavours to develop.

2 Place the chicken in a roasting tin. Coat generously with the coriander and garlic mixture.

3 Sprinkle with more pepper and roast in a preheated oven, 190°C/375°F/Gas Mark 5, on a low shelf for 1½ hours, basting every 20 minutes with the coriander mixture. If the chicken starts to turn brown, cover with foil. Garnish with fresh parsley and serve with the potatoes and carrots.

cook's tip

For pounding small quantities it is best to use a pestle and mortar so as little as possible of the mixture is left in the container.

variation

Any fresh herb can be used in this recipe instead of the coriander. Tarragon or thyme are combine well with chicken.

sweet spiced poussins with walnuts & honey

Baby chickens are ideal for a one or two portion meal, and cook very easily and quickly for a special dinner. If you're cooking for one, a microwave makes cooking even quicker and more convenient.

Serves 2

125 g/4½ oz dried apples, peaches and prunes

120 ml/4 fl oz boiling water

2 baby chickens

25 g/1 oz walnut halves

1 tbsp honey

1 tsp ground allspice

1 tbsp walnut oil

salt and pepper

fresh vegetables and new potatoes, to serve

1 Place the dried fruits in a bowl, cover with the boiling water and leave to stand for about 30 minutes.

2 Cut the chickens in half down the breastbone using a sharp knife, or leave them whole, if you prefer.

3 Mix the fruit and any juices remaining in the bowl with the walnut halves, honey and ground allspice and divide the mixture between two small roasting bags or squares of foil.

4 Brush the chickens with walnut oil and sprinkle with salt and pepper then place on top of the fruit.

5 Close the roasting bags or fold the foil over to enclose the chickens and bake on a baking tray in a preheated oven, 190°C/375°F/Gas Mark 5, for 25–30 minutes or until the juices run clear and not pink when the chicken is pierced in the thickest part with a skewer. To cook in a microwave, use microwave roasting bags and cook on high/ 100% power for 6–7 minutes each, depending on size.

6 Serve hot with fresh vegetables and new potatoes.

cook's tip

Alternative dried fruits that can be used in this recipe are cherries, mangoes or pawpaws.

1

3

5

poussins with herbs & wine

Baby chickens are simple to prepare, take about 30 minutes to roast and can be easily cut in half lengthways with a sharp knife. One baby chicken makes a substantial serving for each person.

Serves 4

5 tbsp fresh brown breadcrumbs

200 g/7 oz fromage frais or low-fat
    crème fraîche

5 tbsp chopped fresh parsley

5 tbsp chopped fresh chives

4 baby chickens

1 tbsp sunflower oil

salt and pepper

675 g/1½ lb young spring vegetables
    such as carrots, courgettes, sugar snap
    peas, sweetcorn and turnips, cut into
    small chunks

120 ml/4 fl oz boiling chicken stock

2 tsp cornflour

150 ml/¼ pint dry white wine

1 In a bowl, mix together the breadcrumbs, one-third of the fromage frais or low-fat crème fraîche and 2 tablespoons each of parsley and chives. Season well with salt and pepper then spoon into the neck ends of the baby chickens. Place the chickens on a rack in a roasting tin, brush with oil and season well.

2

5

2 Roast in a preheated oven, 220°C/425°F/Gas Mark 7, for 30–35 minutes or until the juices run clear, not pink, when the chickens are pierced with a skewer.

3 Place the vegetables in a shallow ovenproof dish in one layer and add half the remaining herbs with the chicken stock. Cover and bake for 25–30 minutes until tender. Strain the vegetables, reserving the cooking juices, and keep warm.

4 Lift the chickens on to a serving plate and skim any fat from the juices in the tin. Add the reserved vegetable juices.

5 Blend the cornflour with the wine and whisk into the sauce with the remaining fromage frais or low-fat crème fraîche. Whisk until boiling, then add the remaining herbs. Season to taste. Spoon the sauce over the chickens and serve with the vegetables.

3

There is nothing more delicious than the juicy flesh and charred skin of chicken that has been grilled over an open fire — after marinating in a flavoursome mixture of oil and herbs or spices. Try an Asian-style mixture of yogurt and aromatic spices, or soy sauce, sesame

oil and fresh ginger root. There are some unusual flavours and innovative tastes,including Chicken Kebabs with Blackberry Sauce, and Marinated Chicken with Satay Sauce, which are attractive whirls of chicken, bacon and basil. Baby

chickens, flavoured with lemon and tarragon in this section, are perfect for grilling or barbecuing. There is also a recipe for Mint Chicken with Mixed Vegetables which combines chicken breasts with a selection of grilled vegetables including courgettes, aubergine and red pepper drizzled with olive oil and served with crusty bread to soak up the delicious juices.

grilled dishes & barbecues

barbecued chicken tikka

Traditionally, chicken tikka is cooked in a clay tandoori oven, but it works well on the barbecue too.

1

Makes 6

4 chicken breasts, skinned and boned

½ tsp salt

4 tbsp lemon or lime juice

150 ml/5 fl oz natural yogurt

2 cloves garlic, crushed

2.5 cm/1 inch piece root ginger,
    peeled and grated

1 tsp ground cumin

1 tsp chilli powder

½ tsp ground coriander

½ tsp ground turmeric

oil or melted butter for brushing

150 ml/5 fl oz natural yogurt

1 tsp mint sauce

2

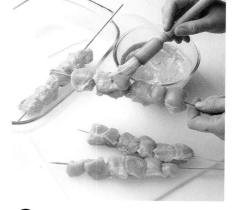

3

1 Cut the chicken into 2.5 cm/1 inch cubes. Sprinkle with the salt and the lemon or lime juice and leave to stand for about 10 minutes.

2 To make the marinade, combine the yogurt, garlic, ginger and ground spices together in a small bowl until well mixed.

3 Thread the cubes of chicken on to skewers. Brush the marinade over the chicken. Cover and leave to marinate in the refrigerator for at least 2 hours, preferably overnight.

4 Barbecue the chicken skewers over hot coals, brushing with oil or butter and turning frequently, for about 15 minutes or until cooked through.

5 Meanwhile, combine the yogurt and mint to make the sauce. Serve the chicken skewers with the mint and yogurt sauce.

variation

Use the marinade to coat chicken portions, such as drumsticks, rather than cubes of chicken, if you prefer. Barbecue over medium hot coals for 30-40 minutes, until the juices run clear when the chicken is pierced with a skewer.

barbecue-style chicken maryland

A barbecue variation of the traditional dish, Chicken Maryland. Serve with sweetcorn — and plenty of serviettes!

Serves 4

8 chicken thighs, skinned and boned

1 tbsp white wine vinegar

1 tbsp lemon juice

1 tbsp golden syrup or clear honey

6 tbsp olive oil

1 clove garlic, crushed

salt and pepper

4 rashers rindless, smoked, streaky bacon

2 bananas

4 cooked sweetcorn and mango chutney,
    to serve

variation

For a quick Maryland-style
dish, omit the marinating
time and cook the chicken
thighs over hot coals for
about 20 minutes, basting
with the marinade. Barbecue
the bananas in their skins
alongside the chicken. Serve
the bananas split open with
a teaspoon of mango chutney.

3

4

1 Cut the chicken into bite-size
pieces. Combine the vinegar, lemon
juice, syrup or honey, oil, garlic and salt
and pepper to taste in a large bowl. Add
the chicken to the marinade and toss
until the chicken is well coated. Cover
and leave to marinate for 1-2 hours.

2 Stretch the bacon rashers with the
back of a knife and then cut each
bacon rasher in half. Cut the bananas
into 2.5 cm/1 inch lengths and brush
them with lemon juice to prevent any
discoloration.

3 Wrap a piece of bacon around each
piece of banana.

4 Remove the chicken from the
marinade, reserving the marinade
for basting. Thread the chicken pieces
and the bacon and banana rolls
alternately on to skewers.

5

5 Barbecue the kebabs over hot
coals for 8–10 minutes until the
chicken is completely cooked. Baste
the kebabs with the marinade and
turn the skewers frequently.

6 Serve with sweetcorn and
mango chutney.

chicken & stuffed pepper kebabs

These kebabs are rather special and are well worth the extra effort needed to prepare them.

Serves 4

3 chicken breasts, skinned and boned

6 tbsp olive oil

4 tbsp lemon juice

½ small onion, grated

1 tbsp fresh, chopped sage

8 tbsp sage and onion stuffing mix

6 tbsp boiling water

2 green peppers, deseeded

1 tbsp olive oil

1 red pepper, deseeded and chopped finely

1 small onion, chopped finely

pinch sugar

210 g/7½ oz can chopped tomatoes

2

4

1 Cut the chicken into evenly sized pieces.

2 Mix the oil, lemon juice, grated onion and sage and pour the mixture into a polythene bag. Add the chicken, seal the bag and shake to coat the chicken. Leave to marinate for at least 30 minutes, shaking the bag occasionally.

3 Place the stuffing mix in a bowl and add the boiling water, stirring to mix well.

4 Cut each pepper into 6 strips, then blanch them in boiling water for 3–4 minutes until softened. Drain and refresh under running water, then drain again.

5 Form about 1 teaspoon of the stuffing mixture into a ball and roll it up in a strip of pepper. Repeat for the remaining stuffing mixture and pepper strips. Thread 3 pepper rolls on to each skewer alternately with pieces of chicken. Leave to chill.

6 To make the sauce, heat the oil in a small pan and fry the red pepper and onion for 5 minutes. Add the sugar and tomatoes and simmer for about 5 minutes. Set aside and keep warm.

7 Barbecue the skewers on an oiled rack over hot coals, basting frequently with the remaining marinade, for about 15 minutes until the chicken is cooked. Serve with the red pepper sauce.

5

sticky chicken & sweetcorn skewers

Chicken wings and corn in a sticky ginger marinade are designed to be eaten with the fingers — there's no other way!

Serves 6

3 cobs fresh sweetcorn

12 chicken wings

2.5cm/1 inch piece fresh ginger root

6 tbsp lemon juice

4 tsp sunflower oil

1 tbsp golden caster sugar

jacket potatoes or salad, to serve

cook's tip

Cut off the wing tips before grilling as they burn very easily. Alternatively, you can cover them with small pieces of foil.

cook's tip

When you are buying fresh sweetcorn, look for plump, tightly packed kernels. If fresh corn is unavailable, you can use thawed, frozen corn instead.

1

2

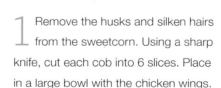

4

1 Remove the husks and silken hairs from the sweetcorn. Using a sharp knife, cut each cob into 6 slices. Place in a large bowl with the chicken wings.

2 Peel and grate the ginger root or chop finely.

3 Mix the ginger root with the lemon juice, sunflower oil and golden caster sugar, then toss with the sweetcorn and chicken to coat.

4 Thread the sweetcorn and chicken wings on to skewers, to make turning easier.

5 Cook the sweetcorn and chicken under a preheated moderately hot grill or barbecue for 15–20 minutes, basting with the gingery glaze and turning frequently until the sweetcorn is golden brown and tender and the chicken is cooked. Serve with jacket potatoes or salad.

cranberry chicken skewers with sesame seeds

The cranberries give the sauce a lovely tart flavour which goes really well with chicken. These Kebabs can be served hot or cold.

2

Serves 8

4 chicken breasts, skinned and boned

4 tbsp dry white wine

1 tbsp light muscovado sugar

2 tbsp sunflower oil

salt and pepper

boiled new potatoes and green salad leaves,
   to serve

SAUCE

175 g/6 oz cranberries

150 ml/5 fl oz cranberry juice drink

2 tbsp light muscovado sugar

100 g/3½ oz sesame seeds

3

5

1 Cut the chicken into 2.5 cm/1 inch pieces. Put the wine, sugar, oil and salt and pepper to taste in a large bowl, stirring to combine. Add the chicken pieces and toss to coat. Leave to marinate for at least 30 minutes, turning the chicken occasionally.

2 To make the sauce, place the ingredients in a small saucepan and bring slowly to the boil, stirring. Simmer gently for 5–10 minutes until the cranberries are soft and pulpy. Taste and add a little extra sugar if wished. Keep warm or leave to chill as required.

3 Remove the chicken pieces from the marinade with a perforated spoon. Thread the chicken pieces on to 8 skewers, spacing them slightly apart to ensure even cooking.

4 Barbecue on an oiled rack over hot coals for 4–5 minutes on each side until just cooked. Brush several times with the marinade during cooking.

5 Remove the chicken skewers from the rack and roll in the sesame seeds. Return to the barbecue and cook for about 1 minute on each side or until the sesame seeds are toasted. Serve with the cranberry sauce, new potatoes and green salad leaves.

variation

Cranberry sauce goes well with all types of poultry. Try it with turkey or guinea fowl.

indian-spiced kebabs

These kebabs are a deliciously different way of serving chicken.
Serve with dhal and chapatis for a really Indian feel.

Serves 6-8

1.5 kg/3 lb 5 oz chicken, boned

½ tsp ground cumin

4 cardamom seeds, crushed

½ tsp ground cinnamon

1 tsp salt

1 tsp fresh ginger root, finely chopped

1 tsp fresh garlic, crushed

½ tsp ground allspice

½ tsp pepper

300 ml/½ pint water

2 tbsp yogurt

2 green chillies

1 small onion

fresh coriander leaves

1 medium egg, beaten

300 ml/½ pint oil

green salad leaves and lemon wedges,
    to garnish

1

2

1 Place the boned chicken in a large
saucepan. Add the ground cumin,
cardamom seeds, ground cinnamon,
salt, ginger, garlic, ground allspice and
pepper and pour in the water. Bring the
mixture to the boil until all of the water
has been absorbed.

2 Put the mixture in a food processor
and grind to form a smooth paste.
Transfer the paste to a mixing bowl. Add
the yogurt and blend together until well
combined.

3 Place the green chillies, onion and
coriander leaves in the food
processor and grind finely. Add to the
chicken mixture and mix well. Add the
beaten egg and mix to combine.

4 Break off 12–15 portions from the
mixture and make small, flat round
shapes in the palm of your hand.

5 Heat the oil in a saucepan and fry
the kebabs gently, in batches,
over a low heat, turning once. Drain
thoroughly on kitchen paper and
serve hot.

3

cook's tip

Indian kebab dishes are
not necessarily cooked on
a skewer; they can also
be served in a dish and
are always dry dishes with
no sauce.

thai-spiced chicken kebabs with lime

Here the chicken is marinated in a delicious aromatic sauce before being threaded on to skewers.

Serves 4

1 tbsp Thai red curry paste

150 ml/5 fl oz canned coconut milk

4 chicken breasts, skinned and boned

1 onion, peeled and cut into wedges

1 large red pepper, deseeded

1 large yellow pepper deseeded

12 kaffir lime leaves

2 tbsp sunflower oil

2 tbsp lime juice

tomato halves, to serve

1 To make the marinade, place the red curry paste in a small pan over medium heat and cook for 1 minute. Add half of the coconut milk to the pan and bring the mixture to the boil. Boil for 2–3 minutes until the liquid has reduced by about two-thirds.

2 Remove the pan from the heat and stir in the remaining coconut milk. Set aside to cool.

3 Cut the chicken into 2.5 cm/1 inch pieces. Stir the chicken into the cold marinade, cover and leave to chill for at least 2 hours.

4 Cut the onion into wedges and the peppers into 2.5 cm/1 inch pieces.

5 Remove the chicken pieces from the marinade and thread them on to skewers, alternating the chicken with the vegetables and lime leaves.

6 Combine the oil and lime juice in a small bowl and brush the mixture over the kebabs. Barbeçue the skewers over hot coals, turning and basting frequently for 10–15 minutes until the chicken is cooked through. Barbecue the tomato halves and serve with the chicken skewers.

cook's tip

Cooking the marinade first intensifies the flavour. It is important to allow the marinade to cool before adding the chicken, or bacteria may breed in the warm temperature. You will find fresh kaffir lime leaves in oriental stores, but if these are unavailable bay leaves can be used instead.

honeyed chicken with mint & yogurt

These tangy lime and honey-coated pieces have a matching sauce or dip based on creamy natural yogurt. They could be served at a barbecue or as a main course for a dinner party.

Serves 6

3 tbsp finely chopped mint

4 tbsp clear honey

4 tbsp lime juice

12 boneless chicken thighs

SAUCE

150 g/5½ oz natural thick yogurt

1 tbsp finely chopped mint

2 tsp finely grated lime rind

green salad, to serve

variation

Use this marinade for chicken kebabs, alternating the chicken with lime and red onion wedges.

cook's tip

Mint can be grown very easily in a garden or window box. It is a useful herb for marinades and salad dressings. Other useful herbs to grow are parsley and basil.

1

2

1 Combine the mint, honey and lime juice in a bowl.

2 Use cocktail sticks to keep the chicken thighs in neat shapes and add the chicken to the marinade, turning to coat evenly.

3 Leave to marinate for at least 30 minutes, preferably overnight. Cook the chicken on a preheated moderately hot barbecue or grill, turning frequently and basting with the marinade. The chicken is cooked if the juices run clear when the chicken is pierced in the thickest part with a skewer.

4

4 Meanwhile, mix together the sauce ingredients.

5 Remove the cocktail sticks and serve the chicken with a salad and the sauce.

chargrilled chicken with ginger & cumin

An Indian-influenced dish that is delicious served with naan bread and a cucumber raita to temper the warmth of the curry.

1

2

Serves 4

4 chicken breasts, skinned and boned

2 tbsp curry paste

1 tbsp sunflower oil

1 tbsp light muscovado sugar

1 tsp ground ginger

½ tsp ground cumin

naan bread and green salad leaves, to serve

CUCUMBER RAITA

¼ cucumber

salt

150 ml/5 fl oz natural yogurt

¼ tsp chilli powder

3

1 Place the chicken breasts between 2 sheets of baking parchment or clingfilm. Pound them with the flat side of a meat mallet or rolling pin to flatten them.

2 Mix together the curry paste, oil, sugar, ginger and cumin in a small bowl. Spread the mixture over both sides of the chicken and set aside until required.

3 To make the raita, peel the cucumber and scoop out the seeds with a spoon. Grate the cucumber flesh, sprinkle with salt, place in a sieve and leave to stand for 10 minutes. Rinse off the salt and squeeze out any moisture by pressing the cucumber with the base of a glass or back of a spoon.

4 Mix the cucumber with the yogurt and stir in the chilli powder. Leave to chill until required.

5 Transfer the chicken to an oiled rack and barbecue over hot coals for 10 minutes, turning once.

6 Warm the naan bread at the side of the barbecue. Serve the chicken with the naan bread and raita and accompanied with fresh green salad leaves.

cook's tip

Flattening the chicken breasts makes them thinner so that they cook more quickly.

chicken quarters with warm mayonnaise

Chicken quarters are barbecued then served with a strongly flavoured garlic mayonnaise, which originated in Provence, France.

Serves 4

4 chicken quarters

2 tbsp oil

2 tbsp lemon juice

2 tsp dried thyme

salt and pepper

AIOLI

5 garlic cloves, crushed

2 egg yolks

120 ml/4 fl oz each olive oil and sunflower oil

2 tsp lemon juice

2 tbsp boiling water

green salad and lemon slices, to serve

1 Using a skewer, prick the chicken quarters in several places then place them in a shallow dish.

2 Combine the oil, lemon juice, thyme and seasoning, then pour over the chicken, turning to coat the chicken evenly. Set aside for 2 hours.

3 To make the aioli, beat together the garlic and a pinch of salt to make a paste. Add the egg yolks and beat well. Gradually add the oils, drop by drop, beating vigorously, until the mayonnaise

1

2

becomes creamy and smooth. Add the oils in a thin steady trickle and continue beating until the aioli is thick. Stir in the lemon juice and season with pepper. Set aside in a warm place.

3

4 Place the chicken on a preheated barbecue and cook for 25–30 minutes. Brush with the marinade and turn the portions to cook evenly. Remove and arrange on a serving plate.

5 Beat the water into the aioli and turn into a warmed serving bowl. Serve the chicken with the aioli, a green salad and lemon slices.

cook's tip

To make a quick aioli, add the garlic to 300 ml/$^1/_2$ pint good quality mayonnaise then place in a bowl over a pan of warm water and beat together. Just before serving add 1-2 tbsp hot water.

fruity glazed chicken

These chicken wings are brushed with a simple barbecue glaze, which can be made in minutes, but the results are sure to delight everyone.

Serves 4

8 chicken wings or 1 chicken cut into 8
   portions

3 tbsp tomato purée

3 tbsp brown fruity sauce

1 tbsp white wine vinegar

1 tbsp clear honey

1 tbsp olive oil

1 clove garlic, crushed (optional)

salad leaves, to serve

variation

This barbecue glaze also makes a very good baste to brush over pork chops.

cook's tip

When poultry is cooked over a very hot barbecue the heat immediately seals in all of the juices, leaving the meat succulent. For this reason you must make sure that the coals are hot enough before starting to barbecue.

1 Remove the skin from the chicken if you want to reduce the fat in the dish.

2 To make the barbecue glaze, place the tomato purée, brown fruity sauce, white wine vinegar, honey, oil and garlic in a small bowl. Stir all of the ingredients together until they are thoroughly blended.

3 Brush the barbecue glaze over the chicken and barbecue over hot coals for 15–20 minutes. Turn the chicken portions over occasionally and baste frequently with the barbecue glaze. If the chicken begins to blacken before it is cooked, raise the rack if possible or move the chicken to a cooler part of the barbecue to slow down the cooking.

4 Transfer the barbecued chicken to warm serving plates and serve with fresh salad leaves.

2

3

1

barbecued chicken with orange & maple syrup

You can use any chicken portions for this recipe. Boned chicken thighs are economical for large barbecue parties, but you could also use wings or drumsticks.

Serves 6

2 boned chicken thighs

5 tbsp maple syrup

1 tbsp caster sugar

grated rind and juice of ½ orange

2 tbsp tomato ketchup

2 tsp Worcestershire sauce

slices of orange and sprig of flat-leaf parsley,
   to garnish

focaccia bread, salad leaves and cherry
   tomatoes, quartered, to serve

1

3

1 Using a sharp knife, make 2–3 slashes in the flesh of the chicken. Place the chicken in a shallow, non-metallic dish.

2 To make the marinade, mix together the maple syrup, sugar, orange rind and juice, ketchup and Worcestershire sauce in a small bowl.

3 Pour the marinade over the chicken, tossing the chicken to coat thoroughly. Cover and leave to chill in the refrigerator until required.

4 Remove the chicken from the marinade, reserving the marinade for basting.

5 Transfer the chicken to the barbecue and cook over hot coals for 20 minutes, turning the chicken and basting with the marinade frequently.

6 Transfer the chicken to serving plates and garnish with slices of orange and a sprig of fresh-leaf parsley. Serve with focaccia bread, fresh salad leaves and cherry tomatoes.

5

cook's tip

If time is short you can omit the marinating time. If you use chicken quarters, rather than the smaller thigh portions, par-boil them for 10 minutes before brushing with the marinade and barbecueing.

spicy chicken wings with chilli salsa

These spicy chicken wings are good served with a chilli salsa and salad. Alternatively, if this is too spicy for your taste, try a sour cream and chive dip.

Serves 4

16 chicken wings

4 tsp paprika

2 tsp ground coriander

1 tsp celery salt

1 tsp ground cumin

½ tsp cayenne pepper

½ tsp salt

1 tbsp oil

2 tbsp red wine vinegar

fresh parsley, to garnish

cherry tomatoes, mixed salad leaves
    and sauce, to serve

1

2

3

Rub this mixture over the wings to coat evenly and set aside, in the refrigerator, for at least 1 hour to allow the flavours to permeate the chicken.

Cook the chicken wings on a preheated barbecue, occasionally brushing with oil, for about 15 minutes, turning often until cooked through. Garnish with fresh parsley and serve with cherry tomatoes, mixed salad leaves and a sauce of your choice.

variation

Although chicken wings do not have much meat on them, they are small and easy to pick up with your fingers which makes them ideal for barbecues. However, they can also be enjoyed fried or roasted.

Wash the chicken wings and pat dry with absorbent paper towels. Remove the wing tips with kitchen scissors.

Mix together the paprika, coriander, celery salt, cumin, cayenne pepper, salt, oil and red wine vinegar.

cook's tip

To save time, you can buy ready-made Cajun spice seasoning to rub over the chicken wings.

mint chicken with mixed vegetables

Grilling is a quick, healthy cooking method, ideal for sealing in the juices and flavour of chicken breasts, and a wonderful way to cook summer vegetables.

Serves 4

1 small aubergine, sliced

salt

2 garlic cloves, crushed

finely grated rind of ½ lemon

1 tbsp chopped fresh mint

6 tbsp olive oil, plus extra for brushing

4 boneless chicken breasts

2 medium courgettes, sliced

1 medium red pepper, quartered

1 small bulb fennel, sliced thickly

1 large red onion, sliced thickly

1 small ciabatta loaf or 1 French baguette,
sliced

1

3

4

1 Place the aubergine slices in a colander and sprinkle with salt. Leave over a bowl to drain for 30 minutes, then rinse and dry. This will get rid of the bitter juices.

2 Mix together the garlic, lemon rind, mint and olive oil and season.

3 Slash the chicken breasts at intervals with a sharp knife. Spoon over about half of the oil mixture and stir to combine.

4 Combine the aubergines and the remaining vegetables, then toss in the remaining oil mixture. Marinate the chicken and vegetables for about 30 minutes.

5 Place the chicken breasts and vegetables on a preheated hot grill or barbecue, turning occasionally, until they are golden brown and tender, or cook on a ridged griddle pan on the hob.

6 Brush the bread slices with olive oil and grill until golden.

7 Drizzle a little olive oil over the chicken and grilled vegetables and serve hot or cold with the crusty bread toasts.

curried chicken with sesame seeds

This is a quick and easy recipe for the grill, perfect for lunch or to eat outdoors on a picnic. They taste good hot or cold.

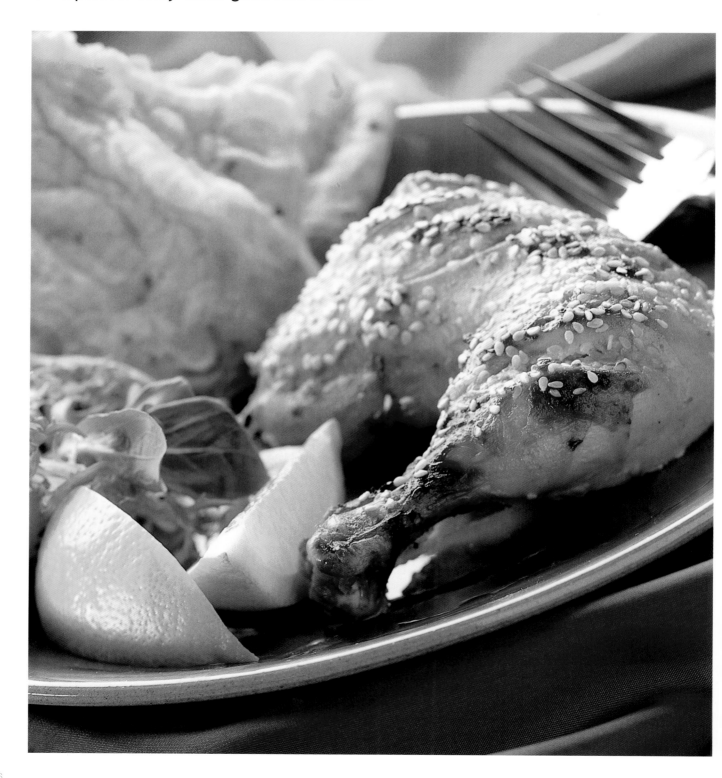

Serves 4

4 chicken quarters

150 g/5½ oz natural yogurt

finely grated rind and juice of 1 small lemon

2 tsp medium-hot curry paste

1 tbsp sesame seeds

salad, naan bread and lemon wedges,
  to serve

1 Remove the skin from the chicken and make cuts in the flesh at intervals with a sharp knife.

2 In a bowl, combine the natural yogurt, lemon rind, lemon juice and curry paste to form a smooth mixture.

3 Spoon the mixture over the chicken and arrange on a foil-lined grill pan or baking tray.

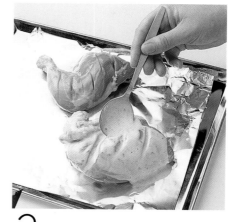

1

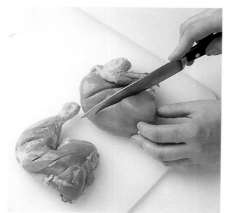

2

3

cook's tip

If you have time, leave the chicken and the sauce in the refrigerator to marinate overnight so the flavours are fully absorbed.

4 Place the chicken quarters under a preheated moderately hot grill and grill for 12–15 minutes, turning once. Grill until golden brown and thoroughly cooked. Just before the end of the cooking time, sprinkle the chicken with the sesame seeds.

5 Serve with a salad, naan bread and lemon wedges.

variation

Poppy seeds, fennel seeds or cumin seeds, or a mixture of all three, can also be used to sprinkle over the chicken.

piquant drumsticks

Chicken drumsticks are marinated to impart a tangy, sweet and sour flavour and a shiny glaze.

Serves 4

8 chicken drumsticks

4 tbsp red wine vinegar

2 tbsp tomato purée

2 tbsp soy sauce

2 tbsp clear honey

1 tbsp Worcestershire sauce

1 garlic clove

good pinch cayenne pepper

sprig of fresh parsley, to garnish

crisp salad, to serve

1

2

3

cook's tip

For a tangy flavour, add the juice of 1 lime to the marinade. While the drumsticks are grilling, check regularly to ensure that they are not burning.

variation

This sweet and sour marinade would also work well with pork or prawns. Thread pork cubes or prawns on to skewers with peppers and button onions.

1 Skin the chicken, if desired, and slash 2–3 times with a sharp knife.

2 Lay the chicken drumsticks side by side in a shallow non-metallic container.

3 Mix the red wine vinegar, tomato purée, soy sauce, honey, Worcestershire sauce, garlic and cayenne pepper together and pour over the chicken drumsticks.

4 Leave to marinate in the refrigerator for 1 hour. Cook the drumsticks on a preheated barbecue for about 20 minutes, brushing with the marinade and turning during cooking. Garnish with parsley and serve with a crisp salad.

chilled chicken with herb vinaigrette

Warm weather calls for lighter eating, and this chilled chicken dish in a subtle herb vinaigrette is ideal for a summer dinner party, or for a picnic.

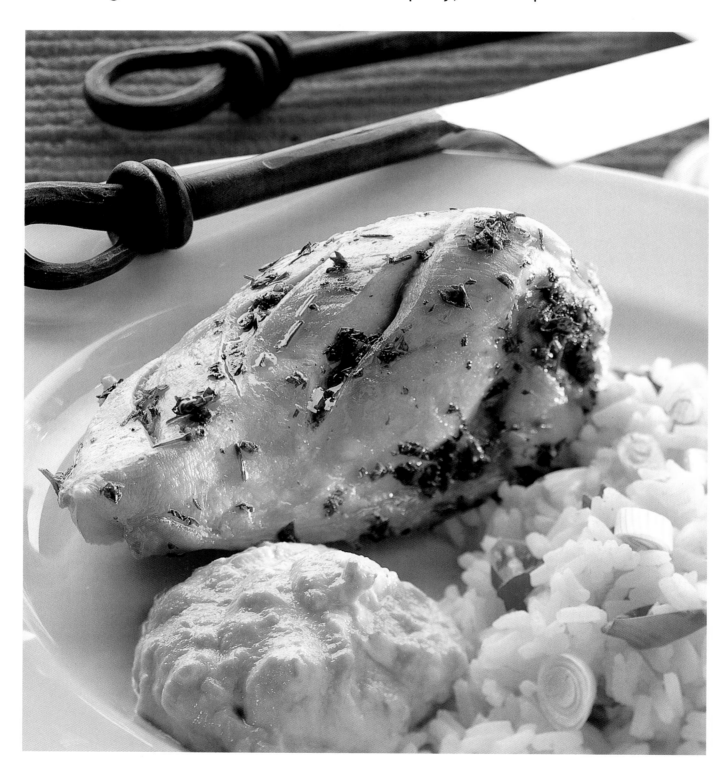

Serves 4

4 part-boned, skinless chicken breasts

6 tbsp olive oil

2 tbsp lemon juice

4 tbsp finely chopped summer herbs,
such as parsley, chives and mint

pepper

1 ripe avocado

125 g/4½ oz low-fatfromage frais

cold rice, to serve

1

1 Using a sharp knife, cut 3–4 deep
slashes in the chicken breasts.

2 Place in a flameproof dish and
brush lightly with a little of the
olive oil.

3 Cook the chicken on a preheated
moderately hot grill turning once
until golden and the juices run clear
when the chicken is pierced in the
thickest part with a skewer.

4 Combine the remaining oil with the
lemon juice and herbs and season
with pepper. Spoon the oil over the
chicken and leave to cool. Chill in the
refrigerator for at least 1 hour.

4

5 Mash the avocado or purée in a
food processor with the fromage
frais. Season with pepper to taste. Serve
the chicken with the avocado sauce and
cold rice.

5

cook's tip

The chicken can be cooked
several hours before you need
it and stored in the
refrigerator until required.

cook's tip

To remove the stone easily
from an avocado, first cut the
avocado in half. Holding one
half securely in your hand,
rap the knife into the stone
so that it becomes embedded in
the stone, then carefully
twist the knife to dislodge
the stone.

spicy caribbean jerk chicken

This is perhaps one of the best known Caribbean dishes. The 'jerk' in the name refers to the hot spicy coating.

Serves 4

4 chicken portions

1 bunch spring onions, trimmed

1–2 Scotch Bonnet chillies, deseeded

1 garlic clove

5 cm/2 inch piece root ginger, peeled and
    roughly chopped

½ tsp dried thyme

½ tsp paprika

¼ tsp ground allspice

pinch ground cinnamon

pinch ground cloves

4 tbsp white wine vinegar

3 tbsp light soy sauce

pepper

cook's tip

As Jamaican cuisine becomes increasingly popular, you will find jars of ready-made jerk marinade, which you can use when time is short. Allow the chicken to marinate for as long as possible for maximum flavour.

variation

You can use milder chillies or even increase the amount of chilli used.

2

3

4

1 Rinse the chicken portions and pat them dry on absorbent kitchen paper. Place them in a shallow dish.

2 Place the spring onions, chillies, garlic, ginger, thyme, paprika, allspice, cinnamon, cloves, wine vinegar, soy sauce and pepper to taste in a food processor and process to make a smooth mixture.

3 Pour the spicy mixture over the chicken. Turn the chicken portions over so that they are well coated in the marinade. Transfer the chicken to the refrigerator and leave to marinate for up to 24 hours.

4 Remove the chicken from the marinade and barbecue over medium hot coals for about 30 minutes, turning the chicken over and basting occasionally with any remaining marinade, until the chicken is cooked through.

5 Transfer the chicken portions to individual serving plates and serve at once.

marmalade chicken drumsticks

These drumsticks are always popular with children — make sure there are plenty of serviettes for wiping sticky fingers or provide finger bowls with a slice of lemon.

Serves 10

10 chicken drumsticks

4 tbsp fine-cut orange marmalade

1 tbsp Worcestershire sauce

grated rind and juice of ½ orange

salt and pepper

30 cherry tomatoes and salad leaves,

   to serve

cook's tip

Par-cooking the chicken is an ideal way of making sure that it is cooked through without becoming overcooked and burned on the outside.

1

1 Using a sharp knife, make 2–3 slashes in the flesh of each chicken drumstick.

2 Bring a large saucepan of water to the boil and add the chicken drumsticks. Cover the pan, return to the boil and cook for 5–10 minutes. Remove the chicken and drain thoroughly.

3 Meanwhile, make the baste. Place the orange marmalade, Worcestershire sauce, orange rind and juice and salt and pepper to taste in a small saucepan. Heat gently, stirring continuously, until the marmalade melts and all of the ingredients are well combined.

4 Brush the baste over the par-cooked chicken drumsticks and transfer them to the barbecue to complete cooking. Barbecue over hot coals for about 10 minutes, turning and basting frequently with the remaining baste.

2

3

5 Carefully thread 3 cherry tomatoes on to each skewer and transfer to the barbecue for 1–2 minutes.

6 Transfer the chicken drumsticks to serving plates. Serve with the cherry tomato skewers and a selection of fresh salad leaves.

chicken & coriander skewers with lemon yogurt

A tangy lemon yogurt is served with this tasty chicken dish.

Serves 4

4 chicken breasts, skinned and boned

1 tsp ground coriander

2 tsp lemon juice

salt and pepper

300 ml/½ pint natural yogurt

1 lemon

2 tbsp chopped, fresh coriander,
   plus sprigs for garnish

oil for brushing

lemon wedges and fresh salad leaves,
   to garnish

cook's tip

These kebabs are delicious
served on a bed of blanched
spinach, which has been
seasoned with salt, pepper
and nutmeg.

variation

Prepare the chicken the day
before it is needed so that it
can marinate overnight. This
will allow the flavours to be
fully absorbed.

1 Cut the chicken into 2.5 cm/1 inch pieces and place them in a shallow, non-metallic dish.

2 Add the coriander, lemon juice, salt and pepper to taste and 4 tbsp of the yogurt to the chicken and mix together until thoroughly combined. Cover and leave to chill for at least 2 hours, preferably overnight.

3

3 To make the lemon yogurt, peel and finely chop the lemon, discarding any pips. Stir the lemon into the yogurt together with the fresh coriander. Leave to chill in the refrigerator until required.

4 Thread the chicken pieces on to skewers. Brush the rack with oil and barbecue the chicken over hot coals for about 15 minutes, basting with the oil.

5 Transfer the chicken kebabs to warm serving plates and garnish with a sprig of fresh coriander, lemon wedges and fresh salad leaves. Serve with the lemon yogurt.

1

2

chicken kebabs with blackberry sauce

This autumnal recipe can be made with fresh-picked wild blackberries from the hedgerow if you're lucky enough to have a good supply.

1

Serves 4

4 chicken breasts or 8 thighs

4 tbsp dry white wine or cider

2 tbsp chopped fresh rosemary

pepper

200 g/7 oz blackberries

1 tbsp cider vinegar

2 tbsp redcurrant jelly

¼ tsp grated nutmeg

rosemary sprigs and blackberries, to garnish

green salad, to serve

2

5

1 Using a sharp knife, cut the chicken into 2.5cm/1 inch pieces and place in a bowl. Sprinkle over the white wine and rosemary, and season well with pepper. Cover and leave to marinate for at least an hour.

2 Drain the chicken, reserving the marinade, and thread the meat on to 8 metal or pre-soaked wooden skewers.

3 Cook on a preheated moderately hot grill for 8–10 minutes, turning occasionally, until golden and evenly cooked.

4 Meanwhile, to make the sauce, place the marinade in a pan with the blackberries and simmer gently until soft. Press the mixture though a sieve using the back of a spoon.

5 Return the blackberry purée to the pan with the cider vinegar and redcurrant jelly and bring to the boil. Boil uncovered until the sauce is reduced by about one-third.

6 Spoon a little blackberry sauce on to each plate and place a chicken skewer on top. Sprinkle with nutmeg and serve hot. Garnish with rosemary and blackberries and serve with a green salad.

cook's tip

If you use canned fruit, omit the redcurrant jelly.

mediterranean chicken kebabs

These unusual chicken kebabs have a wonderful Mediterranean flavour, and the bacon helps keep them moist during cooking.

4

Serves 4

4 skinless, boneless chicken breasts

1 garlic clove, crushed

2 tbsp tomato purée

4 slices smoked back bacon

large handful fresh basil leaves

salt and pepper

oil for brushing

1 Spread out a piece of chicken between two sheets of clingfilm and beat firmly with a rolling pin to flatten the chicken to an even thickness. Repeat with the remaining pieces of chicken.

2 Mix together the crushed garlic and tomato purée until well blended. Spread the mixture evenly over the surface of the chicken.

3 Lay a bacon slice over each piece of chicken, then scatter with the fresh basil leaves. Season well with salt and pepper.

4 Roll up each piece of chicken firmly, then cut into thick slices using a sharp knife.

5 Thread the slices securely on to four skewers, making sure the skewer holds the chicken in a spiral shape.

6 Brush the skewers lightly with oil and cook on a preheated hot barbecue or grill for about 5 minutes, then turn the skewers over and cook for a further 5 minutes, until the chicken is cooked through. Serve the chicken spirals hot with a green salad.

1

3

cook's tip

Flattening the chicken breasts makes them thinner so that they cook more quickly. It also makes them easier to roll.

cook's tip

To complete the Mediterranean theme, serve these kebabs with Parmesan-topped garlic bread.

marinated chicken with satay sauce

This is an ideal sauce to accompany food cooked on the barbecue, and it can be kept warm at the side of the rack.

Serves 4

2 chicken breasts, skinned and boned

MARINADE

4 tbsp sunflower oil

2 cloves garlic crushed

3 tbsp fresh, chopped coriander

1 tbsp caster sugar

½ tsp ground cumin

½ tsp ground coriander

1 tbsp soy sauce

1 red or green chilli, deseeded

salt and pepper

SAUCE

2 tbsp sunflower oil

1 small onion, chopped finely

1 red or green chilli, deseeded and chopped

½ tsp ground coriander

½ tsp ground cumin

8 tbsp peanut butter

8 tbsp chicken stock or water

1 tbsp block coconut

1 Soak 8 wooden skewers in large, shallow dish of cold water for at least 30 minutes. This process will prevent the skewers from burning during barbecueing.

2 Cut the chicken lengthwise into 8 long strips. Thread the strips of chicken, concertina-style, on to the skewers and set aside while you make the marinade.

3 Place the ingredients for the marinade in a food processor and process until smooth.

4 Coat the chicken with the marinade paste, cover and leave to chill in the refrigerator for at least 2 hours.

5 To make the sauce, heat the oil in a small pan and fry the onion and chilli until they are softened but not browned. Stir in the spices and cook for 1 minute. Add the remaining sauce ingredients and cook the mixture gently for 5 minutes. Keep warm at the side of the barbecue.

6 Barbecue the chicken skewers over hot coals for about 10 minutes, basting with any remaining marinade. Serve with the warm sauce.

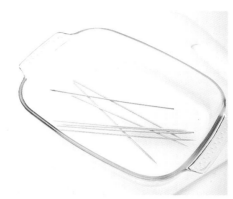

1

2

5

drumstricks in bacon wrappers

Great for barbecues, or for simple summer lunches and picnics, this is an easy and tasty recipe for chicken drumsticks.

Serves 4

10 slices smoked streaky bacon

1 garlic clove, peeled and crushed

3 tbsp wholegrain mustard

4 tbsp fresh brown breadcrumbs

8 chicken drumsticks

1 tbsp sunflower oil

fresh parsley sprigs, to garnish

cook's tip

Don't cook the chicken over the hottest part of the barbecue or the outside may be charred before the centre is cooked.

1

1 Chop two of the bacon slices into small pieces and fry without fat for 3–4 minutes, stirring so that the bacon does not stick to the bottom of the pan. Remove from the heat and stir in the crushed garlic, 2 tablespoons of wholegrain mustard and the breadcrumbs.

2 Carefully loosen the skin from each drumstick with your fingers, being careful not to tear the skin. Spoon a little of the mustard stuffing under each flap of skin, smoothing the skins over firmly afterwards.

2

3 Wrap a bacon rasher around each drumstick, and secure with cocktail sticks.

4 Mix together the remaining mustard and the oil, brush over the chicken drumsticks and cook on a preheated moderately hot barbecue or grill for about 25 minutes, until there is no trace of pink in the juices when the thickest part of the chicken is pierced with a skewer.

3

5 Garnish with the parsley sprigs. The drumsticks may be served hot or cold.

caribbean chicken & mango kebabs

In this recipe, chicken is given a Caribbean flavour. The marinade keeps them moist and succulent during cooking.

Serves 6

750 g/1 lb 10 oz boneless chicken breasts

2 tbsp medium sherry

pepper

3 mangoes

bay leaves

2 tbsp oil

2 tbsp coarsely shredded coconut

crisp salad, to serve

1 Remove the skin from the chicken and cut into 2.5 cm/1 inch cubes and toss in the sherry, with a little pepper.

2 Using a sharp knife, cut the mangoes into 2.5 cm/1 inch cubes, discarding the stone and skin.

3 Thread the chicken, mango cubes and bay leaves alternately on to long skewers, then brush lightly with oil.

1

2

3

4 Grill the skewers on a preheated moderately hot grill for about 8–10 minutes, turning occasionally until golden.

5 Sprinkle the skewers with the coconut and grill for a further 30 seconds. Serve with a crisp salad.

cook's tip

Use mangoes that are ripe but still firm so that they hold together on the skewers during cooking. Another firm fruit that would be suitable is pineapple.

cook's tip

Remember that if you are using metal skewers, they will get very hot, so be sure to use gloves or tongs to turn them. Wooden skewers should be soaked in water for 30 minutes before use to prevent them from burning on the barbeue, and the exposed ends should be covered with pieces of kitchen foil.

skewered spicy tomato chicken

These low-fat, spicy skewers are cooked in a matter of minutes — and they can be assembled ahead of time and stored in the refrigerator until you need them.

Serves 4

500 g/1 lb 2 oz skinless, boneless chicken
    breasts
3 tbsp tomato purée
2 tbsp clear honey
2 tbsp Worcestershire sauce
1 tbsp chopped fresh rosemary
250 g/9 oz cherry tomatoes
couscous or rice, to serve
sprigs of rosemary, to garnish

1

3

1 Using a sharp knife, cut the chicken into 2.5 cm/1 inch chunks and place in a bowl.

2 Mix together the tomato purée, honey, Worcestershire sauce and rosemary. Add to the chicken, stirring to coat evenly.

3 Alternating the chicken pieces and tomatoes, thread them on to eight wooden skewers.

2

4 Spoon over any remaining glaze. Cook under a preheated hot grill for 8–10 minutes, turning occasionally, until the chicken is thoroughly cooked. Serve on a bed of couscous or rice and garnish with sprigs of rosemary.

cook's tip

Couscous is made from semolina that has been made into separate grains. It is very easy to prepare — simply soak it in a bowl of boiling water and then fluff up the grains with a fork. Flavourings such as lemon or nutmeg can be added.

cook's tip

Cherry tomatoes are ideal for barbecues as they can be threaded straight on to skewers. As they are kept whole, the skins keep in the tomatoes' natural juices.

grilled chicken with pesto toasts

This Italian-style dish is richly flavoured with pesto, which is a mixture of basil, olive oil, pine nuts and Parmesan cheese. Either red or green pesto can be used for this recipe.

1

2

Serves 4

8 part-boned chicken thighs

olive oil, for brushing

400 ml/14 fl oz passata

120 ml/4 fl oz green or red pesto sauce

12 slices French bread

90 g/3 oz freshly grated Parmesan cheese

60 g/2 oz pine nuts or flaked almonds

salad leaves, to serve

1 Arrange the chicken in a single layer in a wide flameproof dish and brush lightly with oil. Place under a preheated grill for about 15 minutes, turning occasionally, until golden brown.

2 Pierce the chicken with a skewer to ensure that there is no trace of pink in the juices.

3 Pour off any excess fat. Warm the passata and half the pesto sauce in a small pan and pour over the chicken. Grill for a few more minutes, turning until coated.

4

4 Meanwhile, spread the remaining pesto on to the slices of bread. Arrange the bread over the chicken and sprinkle with the Parmesan cheese. Scatter the pine nuts over the cheese. Grill for 2–3 minutes, or until browned and bubbling. Serve with a selection of salad leaves.

cook's tip

Although leaving the skin on the chicken means that it will have a higher fat content, many people like the rich taste and crispy skin especially when it is blackened by the barbecue. The skin also keeps in the cooking juices.

tarragon poussins with lemon

Spatchcocked baby chickens are complemented by the delicate fragrance of lemon and tarragon and grilled.

Serves 2

2 baby chickens

4 sprigs fresh tarragon

1 tsp oil

25 g/1 oz butter

rind of ½ lemon

1 tbsp lemon juice

1 garlic clove, crushed

salt and pepper

tarragon and lemon slices, to garnish

1 Prepare the baby chickens, turn them breast-side down on a chopping board and cut them through the backbone using kitchen scissors. Crush each bird gently to break the bones so that they lie flat while cooking. Season each with salt.

2 Turn them over and insert a sprig of tarragon under the skin over each side of the breast.

3 Brush the chickens with oil, using a pastry brush, and place under a preheated hot grill about 13 cm/5 inches from the heat. Grill the chickens for about 15 minutes, turning half way, until they are lightly browned.

4 Meanwhile, to make the glaze, melt the butter in a small saucepan, add the lemon rind, lemon juice and garlic and season with salt and pepper.

5 Brush the baby chickens with the glaze and cook for a further 15 minutes, turning them once and brushing regularly so that they stay moist. Garnish the chickens with tarragon and lemon slices and serve with new potatoes.

2

4

1

garlic & lemon poussins with fresh herbs

It is not difficult to spatchcock baby chickens, but it is the best way to cook whole birds on the barbecue.

Serves 2

2 baby chickens, each 450 g/1lb

75 g/2 ¾ oz butter

2 cloves garlic, crushed

2 tbsp chopped, mixed fresh herbs

BASTE

4 tbsp olive oil

2 tbsp lemon juice

2 tbsp chopped, mixed herbs

salt and pepper

cook's tip

Use a combination of whatever fresh herbs you have to hand. Thyme, rosemary, mint, oregano, parsley or coriander are all suitable. If you want to cook a whole chicken in this way double the amount of baste and cook for 40-50 minutes.

3

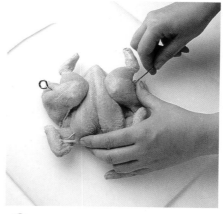

1

1 To spatchcock each chicken, place each bird on its breast and use sharp scissors or poultry shears to cut along the length of the back bone. Open out the bird as much as possible and place it breast-side up on a chopping board. Press down firmly on the breast bone to break it.

2 Mix together the butter, garlic and herbs until well combined. Lift up the skin from the breast of each chicken. Divide the butter equally between the 2 chickens and spread over the breast under the skin.

3 Open out each bird. Thread 2 skewers diagonally through each bird to hold it flat.

4 Mix together the ingredients for the baste in a bowl.

5 Place the birds, bone-side down, over medium hot coals and barbecue for 25 minutes, basting with the lemon and herb baste. Turn the birds over and barbecue, skin-side down, for 15 minutes, basting frequently, or until cooked through.

Because chicken is popular throughout the world, there are countless spicy recipes from Asia, Mexico, the Caribbean, Spain and Japan. Lime juice, peanut, coconut and chilli add the authentic tastes of Thailand to Chilli Coconut Chicken, while Stir-fried Chicken in Cream Sauce is a rich and spicy dish from Northern India with an aromatic sauce made from yogurt, Tikka curry paste, cumin, ginger, chilli and almonds. From Spain comes Chicken & Chorizo with Prawns & Rice with its unusual mixture of chicken and shellfish, together with the famous spicy Spanish sausage, chorizo, slow-cooked in a sauce of garlic, tomatoes and white wine. Lemon & Apricot Chicken is a creative modern dish that would be perfect for any special occasion. The chicken is stuffed with dried apricots, coated in a yogurt, cumin and turmeric sauce

and served with nutty rice. There is even a dish from Japan, Japanese Chicken & Vegetables, a simple dish of fried chicken slices with peppers, spring onions and bean sprouts, served with a mirin dipping sauce.

dishes for
entertaining

chicken, carrot & noodle stir-fry

The chicken and noodles are cooked and then a flavoured egg mixture is tossed into the dish to coat the noodles and meat in this delicious recipe.

Serves 4

250 g/9 oz egg noodles

450 g/1 lb chicken thighs

2 tbsp groundnut oil

100 g/3½ oz carrots, sliced

3tbsp oyster sauce

2 eggs

3 tbsp cold water

variation

Flavour the eggs with soy sauce or hoisin sauce as an alternative to the oyster sauce, if you prefer.

1 Place the egg noodles in a large bowl or dish. Pour enough boiling water over the noodles to cover and leave to stand for 10 minutes.

2 Meanwhile, remove the skin from the chicken thighs. Cut the chicken flesh into small pieces, using a sharp knife.

3 Heat the groundnut oil in a large preheated wok.

4 Add the pieces of chicken and the carrot slices to the wok and stir-fry the mixture for about 5 minutes.

5 Drain the noodles thoroughly. Add the noodles to the wok and stir-fry for a further 2–3 minutes or until the noodles are heated through.

2

4

6 Beat together the oyster sauce, eggs and of cold water. Drizzle the mixture over the noodles and stir-fry for a further 2–3 minutes or until the eggs set. Transfer to warm serving bowls and serve hot.

1

chicken, pepper & mushroom stir-fry

Ready-made yellow bean sauce is available from large supermarkets and Chinese food stores. It is made from yellow soya beans and is quite salty in flavour.

6

7

Serves 4

450 g/1 lb skinless, boneless

   chicken breasts

1 egg white, beaten

1 tbsp cornflour

1 tbsp rice wine vinegar

1 tbsp light soy sauce

1 tsp caster sugar

3 tbsp vegetable oil

1 garlic clove, crushed

1 cm/½ inch piece fresh root ginger, grated

1 green pepper, seeded and diced

2 large mushrooms, sliced

3 tbsp yellow bean sauce

yellow or green pepper strips, to garnish

1   Trim any fat from the chicken and cut the meat into 2.5 cm/1 inch cubes.

2   Mix the egg white and cornflour in a shallow bowl. Add the chicken and turn in the mixture to coat. Set aside for 20 minutes.

3   Mix the vinegar, soy sauce and sugar in a bowl.

4   Remove the chicken from the egg white mixture.

5   Heat the oil in a preheated wok, add the chicken and stir-fry for 3–4 minutes, until golden brown. Remove the chicken from the wok with a slotted spoon, set aside and keep warm.

6   Add the garlic, ginger, pepper and mushrooms to the wok and stir-fry for 1–2 minutes.

7   Add the yellow bean sauce and cook for 1 minute. Stir in the vinegar mixture and return the chicken to the wok. Cook for 1–2 minutes and serve hot, garnished with pepper strips.

variation

Black bean sauce would work equally well with this recipe. Although this would affect the appearance of the dish, as it is much darker in colour, the flavours would be compatible.

1

stir-fried chicken strips & golden rice

This is a really colourful main meal or side dish which tastes just as good as it looks.

Serves 4

350 g/12 oz long-grain white rice

1 tsp turmeric

2 tbsp sunflower oil

350 g/12 oz skinless, boneless chicken
   breasts or thighs, sliced

1 red pepper, deseeded and sliced

1 green pepper, deseeded and sliced

1 green chilli, deseeded and finely chopped

1 medium carrot, coarsely grated

150 g/5½ oz beansprouts

6 spring onions, sliced, plus extra to garnish
   (optional)

2 tbsp soy sauce

1

4

7

1 Place the rice and turmeric in a large saucepan of lightly salted water and cook until the grains of rice are just tender, about 10 minutes. Drain the rice thoroughly and press out any excess water with double thickness paper towels.

2 Heat the sunflower oil in a large preheated wok.

3 Add the strips of chicken to the wok and stir-fry over a high heat until the chicken is just beginning to turn a golden colour.

4 Add the peppers and chilli to the wok and stir-fry for 2–3 minutes.

5 Add the rice to the wok, a little at a time, tossing well after each addition until well combined.

6 Add the carrot, beansprouts and spring onions to the wok and stir-fry for a further 2 minutes.

7 Drizzle with the soy sauce and mix well.

8 Garnish with extra spring onions, if wished and serve at once.

variation

Use pork marinated in hoisin sauce instead of the chicken, if you prefer.

fiery chicken & sherry stir-fry

This is quite a hot dish, using fresh chillies. If you prefer a milder dish, halve the number of chillies used.

Serves 4

350 g/12 oz skinless, boneless lean chicken

½ tsp salt

1 egg white, lightly beaten

2 tbsp cornflour

4 tbsp vegetable oil

2 garlic cloves, crushed

1 cm/½ inch piece fresh root ginger, grated

1 red pepper, seeded and diced

1 green pepper, seeded and diced

2 fresh red chillies, chopped

2 tbsp light soy sauce

1 tbsp dry sherry or Chinese rice wine

1 tbsp wine vinegar

1 Cut the chicken into cubes and place in a mixing bowl. Add the salt, egg white, cornflour and 1 tablespoon of the oil. Turn the chicken in the mixture to coat thoroughly.

2 Heat the remaining oil in a preheated wok. Add the garlic and ginger and stir-fry for 30 seconds.

3 Add the chicken pieces to the wok and stir-fry for 2–3 minutes, or until browned.

4 Stir in the peppers, chillies, soy sauce, sherry or Chinese rice wine and wine vinegar and cook for a further 2–3 minutes, until the chicken is cooked through. Transfer to a warm serving dish and serve.

4

1

3

variation

This recipe works well if you use 350 g/12 oz lean steak, cut into thin strips or 450 g/1 lb raw prawns instead of the chicken.

cook's tip

When preparing chillies, wear rubber gloves to prevent the juices from burning and irritating your hands. Be careful not to touch your face, especially your lips or eyes, until you have washed your hands.

stir-fried chicken in cream sauce

A simple and mouth-watering dish with a lovely thick sauce,
this makes an impressive centrepiece for a dinner party.

Serves 4-6

100 g/3½ oz unsalted butter

1 tbsp oil

2 medium onions, finely chopped

1 tsp fresh ginger root, finely chopped

2 tsp garam masala

2 tsp ground coriander

1 tsp chilli powder

1 tsp black cumin seeds

1 tsp fresh garlic, crushed

1 tsp salt

3 whole green cardamoms

3 whole black peppercorns

150 ml/5 fl oz natural yogurt

2 tbsp tomato purée

8 chicken pieces, skinned

150 ml/¼ pint water

2 whole bay leaves

150 ml/5 fl oz single cream

fresh coriander leaves and 2 green chillies,

    chopped, to garnish

2

2

1 Heat the butter and oil in a large frying pan. Add the onions and fry until golden brown, stirring. Reduce the heat.

2 Crush the fresh ginger and place in a bowl. Add the garam masala, ground coriander, ginger, chilli powder, black cumin seeds, garlic, salt, cardamoms and black peppercorns and blend. Add the yogurt and tomato purée and stir to combine.

3 Add the chicken pieces to the yogurt and spice mixture and mix to coat well.

4 Add the chicken to the onions in the pan and stir-fry vigorously, making semi-circular movements, for 5–7 minutes.

5 Add the water and the bay leaves to the mixture in the pan and leave to simmer for 30 minutes, stirring occasionally.

6 Add the cream and cook for a further 10-15 minutes.

7 Garnish with fresh coriander leaves and chillies and serve hot.

2

peppered chicken stir-fry

Using black pepper instead of chilli powder produces a milder curry. This recipe is basically a stir-fry and can be prepared in a short time. The dish goes well with fried corn and peas.

Serves 4-6

8 chicken thighs

1 tsp fresh ginger root, finely chopped

1 tsp fresh garlic, crushed

1 tsp salt

1½ tsp pepper

150 ml/¼ pint oil

1 green pepper, roughly sliced

150 ml/¼ pint water

2 tbsp lemon juice

FRIED CORN & PEAS

50 g/2 oz unsalted butter

200 g/8 oz frozen sweetcorn

200 g/8 oz frozen peas

½ tsp salt

½ tsp chilli powder

1 tbsp lemon juice

fresh coriander leaves, to garnish

1

2

6

1 Using a sharp knife, bone the chicken thighs, if you prefer.

2 Combine the ginger, garlic, salt and coarsely ground black pepper together in a mixing bowl.

3 Add the chicken pieces to the black pepper mixture and set aside until required.

4 Heat the oil in a large pan. Add the chicken pieces and stir-fry for 10 minutes.

5 Reduce the heat and add the green pepper and the water to the pan. Leave the mixture to simmer for 10 minutes, then sprinkle over the lemon juice.

6 Meanwhile, make the fried corn and peas. Melt the butter in a large frying pan. Add the sweetcorn and peas and fry, stirring occasionally, for about 10 minutes. Add the salt and chilli powder and fry for a further 5 minutes.

7 Sprinkle over the lemon juice and garnish with fresh coriander leaves.

8 Transfer the chicken and pepper mixture to serving plates and serve with the fried corn and peas.

chicken & beanspout salad with peanut dressing

The spicy peanut dressing served with this salad may be prepared in advance and left to chill a day before required.

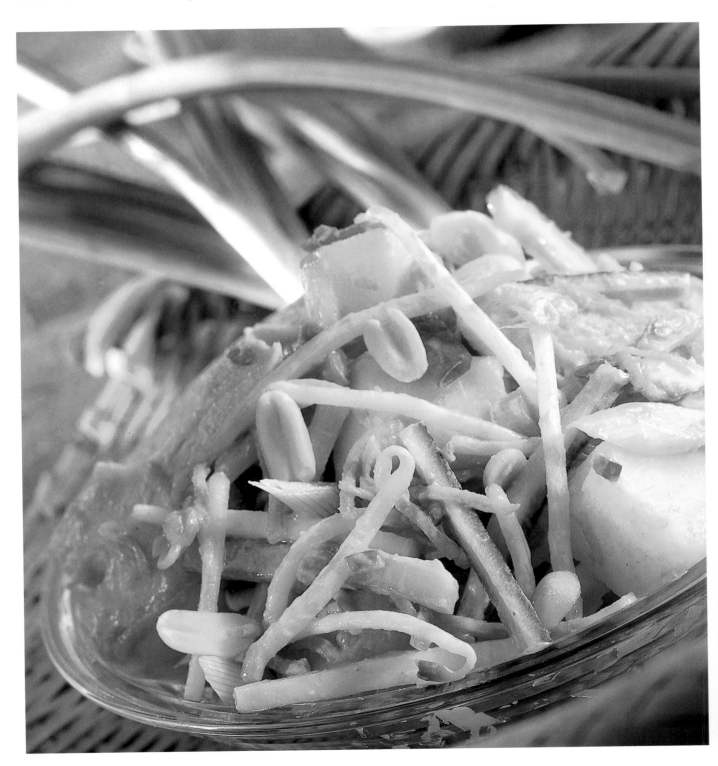

Serves 4

4 large waxy potatoes, diced

300 g/10½ oz fresh pineapple, diced

2 carrots, grated

175 g/6 oz beansprouts

1 bunch spring onions, sliced

1 large courgette, cut into matchsticks

3 celery sticks, cut into matchsticks

175 g/6 oz unsalted peanuts

2 cooked chicken breast fillets, about
    125 g/4½ oz each, sliced

DRESSING

6 tbsp crunchy peanut butter

6 tbsp olive oil

2 tbsp light soy sauce

1 red chilli, chopped

2 tsp sesame oil

4 tsp lime juice

lime wedges, to garnish

3

4

5

1 Cook the diced potatoes in a saucepan of boiling water for 10 minutes or until tender. Drain and leave to cool.

2 Transfer the cooled potatoes to a salad bowl.

3 Add the pineapple, carrots, beansprouts, spring onions, courgette, celery, peanuts and sliced chicken to the potatoes. Toss well to mix all the salad ingredients together.

4 To make the dressing, put the peanut butter in a small bowl and gradually whisk in the olive oil and light soy sauce.

5 Stir in the chopped red chilli, sesame oil and lime juice. Mix until well combined.

cook's tip

Unsweetened canned pineapple may be used in place of the fresh pineapple for convenience. If only sweetened canned pineapple is available, drain it and rinse under cold running water before using.

6 Pour the spicy dressing over the salad and toss lightly to coat all of the ingredients. Serve the salad immediately, garnished with lime wedges.

chilli & peanut chicken

This quick dish has many variations, but this version includes the classic combination of peanuts, chicken and chillies, blending together to give a wonderfully flavoured dish.

Serves 4

300 g/10½ oz skinless, boneless
  chicken breast
2 tbsp peanut oil
125 g/4½ oz shelled peanuts
1 fresh red chilli, sliced
1 green pepper, seeded and cut into strips
fried rice, to serve

SAUCE
150 ml/¼ pint chicken stock
1 tbsp Chinese rice wine or dry sherry
1 tbsp light soy sauce
1½ tsp light brown sugar
2 garlic cloves, crushed
1 tsp grated fresh root ginger
1 tsp rice wine vinegar
1 tsp sesame oil

1 Trim any fat from the chicken and cut the meat into 2.5 cm/1 inch cubes. Set aside.

2 Heat the peanut oil in a preheated wok. Add the peanuts and stir-fry for 1 minute. Remove the peanuts with a slotted spoon and set aside.

3 Add the chicken to the wok and cook for 1–2 minutes. Stir in the chilli and green pepper and cook for 1 minute. Remove from the wok with a slotted spoon and set aside.

4 Put half of the peanuts in a food processor and process until almost smooth. Alternatively, place them in a plastic bag and crush them with a rolling pin.

5 To make the sauce, add the chicken stock, Chinese rice wine or dry sherry, soy sauce, sugar, garlic, ginger and rice wine vinegar to the wok.

6 Heat the sauce without boiling and stir in the peanuts, chicken, chilli and pepper.

7 Sprinkle the sesame oil into the wok, stir and cook for 1 minute. Serve hot with fried rice.

cook's tip

If necessary, process the peanuts with a little of the stock in step 4 to form a softer paste.

3

4

6

chicken parcels in red wine sauce

There is a delicious surprise inside these chicken breast parcels!

Serves 4

4 chicken breasts, skin removed

100 g/3½ oz full fat soft cheese, flavoured with herbs and garlic

8 slices Parma ham

150 ml/5 fl oz red wine

150 ml/5 fl oz chicken stock

1 tbsp brown sugar

variation

Try adding 2 finely chopped sun-dried tomatoes to the soft cheese in step 2, if you prefer.

1

3

2

1 Using a sharp knife, make a horizontal slit along the length of each chicken breast to form a pocket.

2 Beat the cheese with a wooden spoon to soften it. Spoon the cheese into the pocket of the chicken breasts.

3 Wrap 2 slices of Parma ham around each chicken breast and secure in place with a length of string.

4 Pour the wine and chicken stock into a large frying pan and bring to the boil. When the mixture is just starting to boil, add the sugar and stir to dissolve.

5 Add the chicken breasts to the mixture in the frying pan. Leave to simmer for 12–15 minutes or the chicken is tender and the juices run clear when a skewer is inserted into the thickest part of the meat.

6 Remove the chicken from the pan, set aside and keep warm.

7 Reheat the sauce and boil until reduced and thickened. Remove the string from the chicken and cut into slices. Pour the sauce over the chicken to serve.

warm spiced chicken with almonds & rice

This tasty chicken dish combines warm spices and almonds and is spiked with anise.

Serves 4

25 g/1 oz butter

7 tbsp vegetable oil

4 skinless, boneless chicken breasts,
  cut into 4 x 2 cm/2 x1 inch pieces

1 medium onion, roughly chopped

2 cm/1 inch piece fresh ginger root

3 garlic cloves, peeled

25 g/1 oz blanched almonds

1 large red pepper, roughly chopped

1 tbsp ground cumin

2 tsp ground coriander

1 tsp ground turmeric

pinch cayenne pepper

½ tsp salt

150 ml/¼ pint water

3 star anise

2 tbsp lemon juice

pepper

flaked almonds, to garnish

rice, to serve

1

1 Heat the butter and 1 tablespoon of oil in a frying pan, add the chicken pieces and cook for 5 minutes until golden. Transfer the chicken pieces to a plate and keep warm until required.

2 Combine the onion, ginger, garlic, almonds, red pepper, cumin, coriander, turmeric, cayenne pepper and salt in a food processor or liquidiser. Blend to form a smooth paste.

3 Heat the remaining oil in a large saucepan or deep frying pan. Add the paste and fry for 10–12 minutes.

4 Add the chicken pieces, the water, star anise, lemon juice and pepper. Cover, reduce the heat and simmer gently for 25 minutes or until the chicken is tender, stirring a few times during cooking.

5 Transfer the chicken to a serving dish, sprinkle with the flaked almonds and serve with individual rice moulds.

2

4

spiced chicken with pilau rice

This warming, rich and spicy dish is based on the traditional cooking style of Northern India, using chicken on the bone.

Serves 4

4 skinless chicken drumsticks

4 skinless chicken thighs

150 ml/¼ pint natural yogurt

4 tbsp tikka curry paste

2 tbsp sunflower oil

1 medium onion, sliced thinly

1 garlic clove, crushed

1 tsp ground cumin

1 tsp finely chopped fresh ginger root

½ tsp chilli paste

4 tsp chicken stock

2 tbsp ground almonds

salt

fresh coriander, to garnish

pilau rice, pickles and poppadums, to serve

variation

If you prefer, use boneless chicken breasts instead of legs, and cut into large chunks for cooking.

2

1 Slash the chicken fairly deeply at intervals with a sharp knife and place in a large bowl.

2 Mix together the natural yogurt and curry paste and stir into the chicken, tossing to coat evenly. Cover and chill for at least 1 hour.

3 Heat the oil in a large pan and fry the onion and garlic for 4–5 minutes until softened but not browned.

4 Stir in the cumin, ginger and chilli paste and cook gently for 1 minute.

5 Add the chicken pieces and fry gently, turning from time to time, for about 10 minutes or until evenly browned. Stir in any remaining marinade with the stock and almonds.

6 Cover the pan and simmer gently for a further 15 minutes or until the chicken is completely cooked and tender.

7 Season to taste with a little salt. Garnish the chicken with coriander and serve with pilau rice, pickles and poppadums.

3

4

chicken & kidney bean tortillas

Serve these easy-to-prepare tortillas to friends or as a special family supper. The chicken filling has a mild, mellow spicy heat and a fresh salad makes a perfect accompaniment.

Serves 4

2 tbsp oil

8 skinless, boneless chickenthighs, sliced

1 onion, chopped

2 garlic cloves, chopped

1 tsp cumin seeds, roughly crushed

2 large dried chillies, sliced

400 g/14 oz can tomatoes

400 g/14 oz can red kidneybeans, drained

150 ml/¼ pint chicken stock

2 tsp sugar

salt and pepper

lime wedges, to garnish

TO SERVE

1 large ripe avocado

1 lime

8 soft tortillas

250 ml/9 fl oz thick yogurt

1

2

3

1 Heat the oil in a large frying pan or wok, add the chicken and fry for 3 minutes until golden. Add the onion and fry for 5 minutes, stirring until browned. Add the garlic, cumin and chillies, with their seeds, and cook for about 1 minute.

2 Add the tomatoes, kidney beans, stock, sugar and salt and pepper to taste. Bring to the boil, breaking up the tomatoes. Cover and simmer for 15 minutes. Remove the lid and cook for 5 minutes, stirring occasionally until the sauce has thickened.

3 Halve the avocado, discard the stone and scoop out the flesh on to a plate. Mash the avocado with a fork. Cut half of the lime into 8 thin wedges. Squeeze the juice from the remaining lime over the avocado.

4 Warm the tortillas following the instructions on the packet. Put two tortillas on each serving plate, fill with the chicken mixture and top with spoonfuls of avocado and yogurt. Garnish the tortillas with lime wedges.

variation

For a vegetarian filling, replace the chicken with 400 g/14 oz canned pinto or cannellini beans and use vegetable stock instead of the chicken stock.

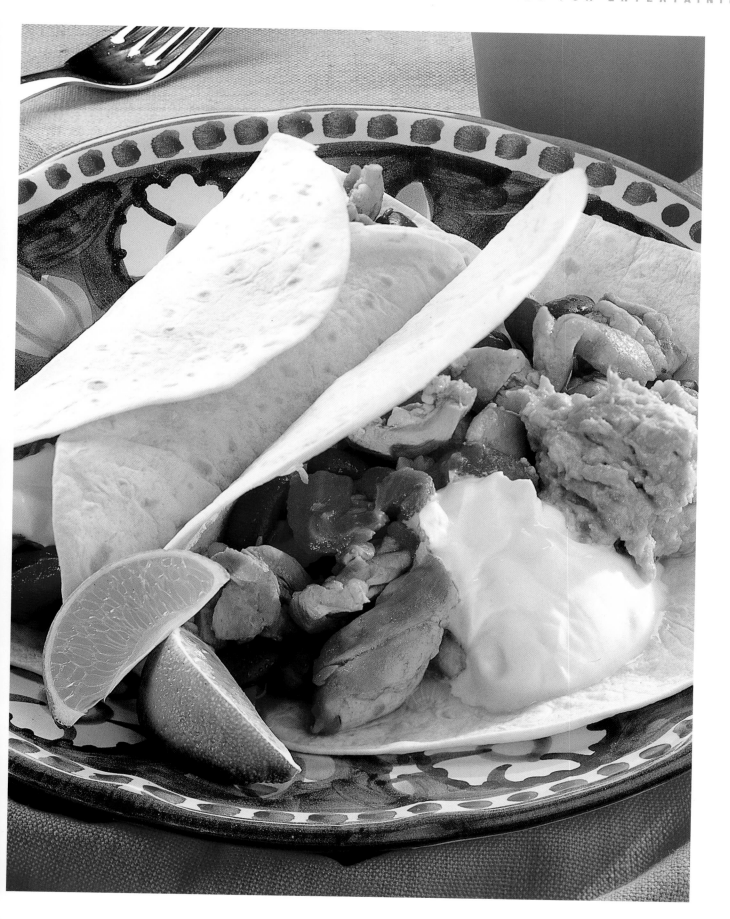

chilli & onion chicken with mixed spices

This dish represents one of the rare occasions when we do not use yogurt to cook chicken. It has a lovely flavour and is perfect served with rice. It also freezes very well.

Serves 4

300 ml/½ pint oil

4 medium onions, finely chopped

1½ tsp fresh ginger root, finely chopped

1½ tsp garam masala

1½ tsp fresh garlic, crushed

1 tsp chilli powder

1 tsp ground coriander

3 whole cardamoms

3 peppercorns

3 tbsp tomato purée

8 chicken thighs, skinned

300 ml/½ pint water

2 tbsp lemon juice

1 green chilli

fresh coriander leaves

green chilli strips, to garnish

cook's tip

A dish of meat cooked with plenty of onions is called a Do Pyaza. This curry definitely improves if made in advance and then reheated before serving. This develops the flavours and makes them deeper.

1

1 Heat the oil in a large frying pan. Add the onions and fry, stirring occasionally, until golden brown.

2 Reduce the heat and add the ginger, garam masala, garlic, chilli powder, ground coriander, whole cardamoms and the peppercorns, stirring to mix.

3 Add the tomato purée to the mixture in the frying pan and stir-fry for 5–7 minutes.

4 Add the chicken thighs to the pan and toss to coat with the spice mixture.

5 Pour the water into the saucepan, cover and leave to simmer for 20–25 minutes.

3

4

6 Add the lemon juice, green chilli and coriander to the mixture, and combine.

7 Transfer the chicken and onions to serving plates, garnish with chilli strips and serve hot.

golden chicken

A spicy, Indian-style coating is baked around lean chicken to give a full flavour. Serve hot or cold with a tomato, cucumber and coriander relish.

Serves 4

1 garlic clove, crushed

2.5 cm/1 inch piece root ginger, finely
    chopped

1 fresh green chilli, deseeded and finely
    chopped

6 tbsp low-fat natural yogurt

1 tbsp tomato purée

1 tsp ground turmeric

1 tsp garam masala

1 tbsp lime juice

salt and pepper

4 boneless, skinless chicken breasts, each
    125 g/4½ oz

wedges of lime or lemon, to serve

RELISH

4 medium tomatoes

¼ cucumber

1 small red onion

2 tbsp fresh coriander, chopped

variation

The spicy yogurt coating would work just as well if spread on a chunky white fish such as cod fillet. The cooking time should be reduced to 15-20 minutes.

1

2

1 Preheat the oven to 190°C/ 375°F/Gas Mark 5. In a small bowl mix together the garlic, ginger, chilli, yogurt, tomato purée, turmeric, garam masala, lime juice and seasoning.

2 Wash and pat dry the chicken breasts and place them on a baking sheet. Brush or spread the spicy yogurt mix over the chicken and bake in the oven for 30–35 minutes until the meat is tender and cooked through.

3 Meanwhile, make the relish. Finely chop the tomatoes, cucumber and onion and mix together with the coriander. Season, cover and chill until required.

4 Drain the cooked chicken on absorbent kitchen paper and serve hot with the relish. Or, allow to cool, chill for at least 1 hour and serve sliced as part of a salad.

3

chicken & chorizo with prawns & rice

This unusual dish, with its mixture of chicken and shellfish, is typically Spanish. The basis of this recipe is sofrito a slow-cooked mixture of onion and tomato in olive oil, with garlic and peppers.

Serves 4

4 chicken quarters

1 tbsp olive oil

1 red pepper

1 medium onion

2 garlic cloves, crushed

400 g/14 oz can chopped tomatoes

200 ml/7 fl oz dry white wine

4 tbsp chopped fresh oregano

salt and pepper

125 g/4½ oz chorizo sausage

125 g/4½ oz peeled prawns

rice, to serve

cook's tip

Chorizo is a spicy Spanish sausage made with pork and a hot pepper such as cayenne or pimento. It is available from large supermarkets and specialist butchers.

1

2

4

1 Remove the skin from the chicken quarters. Heat the oil in a wide, heavy pan and fry the chicken, turning occasionally until golden brown.

2 Using a sharp knife, deseed and slice the pepper and peel and slice the onion. Add the pepper and onion to the pan and fry gently to soften.

3 Add the garlic with the tomatoes, wine and oregano. Season well with salt and pepper, then bring to the boil, cover and simmer gently for 45 minutes or until the chicken is tender and the juices run clear when the thickest part of the chicken is pierced with a skewer.

4 Thinly slice the chorizo and add to the pan together with the prawns, then simmer for a further 5 minutes. Adjust the seasoning to taste and serve with rice.

tropical chicken

This exotic dish can be made with any cut of chicken, but drumsticks are best for quick and even cooking. Grated fresh coconut adds a delicious, tropical flavour.

Serves 4

8 skinless chicken drumsticks

2 limes

1 tsp cayenne pepper

2 medium mangoes

1 tbsp sunflower oil

2 tbsp dark muscovado sugar

lime wedges and fresh parsley, to garnish

2 tbsp coarsely grated coconut (optional),
   to serve

1 With a sharp knife, slash the
chicken drumsticks at intervals then
place the chicken in a large bowl.

2 Grate the rind from the limes and
set aside.

3 Squeeze the juice from the limes
and sprinkle over the chicken with
the cayenne pepper. Cover and chill in
the refrigerator for at least two hours or
overnight.

4 Peel the mangoes and chop in half.
Discard the stone and cut the flesh
into slices.

3

4

5

5 Drain the chicken drumsticks using
a slotted spoon and reserve the
juice. Heat the oil in a wide heavy pan
and sauté the chicken drumsticks,
turning frequently, until golden. Stir in
the marinade, lime rind, mango slices
and the dark muscovado sugar.

6 Cover the pan and simmer gently,
stirring occasionally, for 15 minutes,
or until the chicken juices run clear
when pierced with a skewer. Sprinkle
with grated coconut, if using, and
garnish with lime wedges and fresh
parsley.

variation

When buying mangoes, bear in
mind that the skin of ripe
mangoes varies in colour from
green to pinky-red and the
flesh from pale yellow to
bright orange. Choose mangoes
which yield to gentle
pressure.

lemon & apricot chicken

Spiced chicken legs are partially boned and packed with dried apricots for an intense fruity flavour. A golden, spiced, low-fat yogurt coating keeps the chicken moist and tender.

Serves 4

4 large, skinless chicken leg quarters

finely grated rind of 1 lemon

salt and pepper

200 g/7 oz ready-to-eat dried apricots

1 tbsp ground cumin

1 tsp ground turmeric

125 g/4½ oz low-fat natural yogurt

TO SERVE

250 g/9 oz brown rice

2 tbsp flaked hazelnuts or almonds, toasted

2 tbsp sunflower seeds, toasted

lemon wedges and a fresh salad

2

4

3

brush this mixture over the chicken to coat evenly. Place the chicken in an ovenproof dish or roasting tin and bake in a preheated oven, 190°C/375°F/Gas Mark 5, for about 35–40 minutes, or until the juices run clear, not pink, when the chicken is pierced through the thickest part with a skewer.

1 Remove any excess fat from the chicken legs.

2 Use a small sharp knife carefully to cut the flesh away from the thigh bone.

3 Scrape the meat away down as far as the knuckle. Grasp the thigh bone firmly and twist it to break it away from the drumstick.

4 Open out the boned part of the chicken and sprinkle with lemon rind and pepper. Pack the dried apricots into each piece of chicken. Fold over to enclose, and secure with cocktail sticks.

5 Mix together the cumin, turmeric, yogurt and salt and pepper, then

6 Meanwhile, cook the rice in boiling, lightly salted water until just tender, then drain well. Stir the hazelnuts and sunflower seeds into the rice. Serve the chicken with the nutty rice, lemon wedges and a fresh salad.

grilled tandoori chicken

In India, tandoori chicken is traditionally cooked in a tandoor (clay) oven. Alternatively, you can pre-heat the grill to a very high temperature then lower it to medium to cook this dish.

Serves 4

8 chicken drumsticks, skinned

150 ml/5 fl oz natural yogurt

1½ tsp fresh ginger root, finely chopped

1½ tsp fresh garlic, crushed

1 tsp chilli powder

2 tsp ground cumin

2 tsp ground coriander

1 tsp salt

½ tsp red food colouring

1 tbsp tamarind paste

150 ml/¼ pint water

150 ml/¼ pint oil

lettuce leaves, onion rings, sliced tomatoes
and lemon wedges, to serve

cook's tip

Shop-bought naan bread and
Raita will complement the dish
perfectly.

2

1 Make 2–3 slashes in each piece of chicken.

2 Place the yogurt in a bowl. Add the ginger, garlic, chilli powder, ground cumin, ground coriander, salt and red food colouring and blend together until well combined.

3 Add the chicken to the yogurt and spice mixture and mix to coat well. Leave the chicken to marinate in the refrigerator for a minimum of 3 hours.

4 In a separate bowl, mix the tamarind paste with the water and fold into the yogurt and spice mixture. Toss the chicken pieces in this mixture and set aside to marinate for a further 3 hours.

5 Transfer the chicken pieces to a heatproof dish and brush the chicken with oil. Cook the chicken under a pre-heated medium-hot grill for 30–35 minutes, turning the chicken pieces occasionally and basting with the remaining oil.

6 Arrange the chicken on a bed of lettuce and garnish with onion rings, sliced tomatoes and lemon wedges.

3

5

one pot chicken

This complete main course is cooked in one saucepan for simplicity.
If you're cooking for one, simply halve the ingredients; the cooking time
should stay the same.

Serves 2

1 tbsp sunflower oil

4 chicken thighs

1 small onion, diced

2 sticks celery, diced

1 small green pepper, diced

90 g/3 oz long grain rice

300 ml/½ pint chicken stock

1 small red chilli

250 g/9 oz okra

15 ml/1 tbsp tomato purée

salt and pepper

1 Heat the oil in a wide pan and fry the chicken until golden. Remove the chicken from the pan using a slotted spoon. Stir in the onion, celery and pepper and fry for 1 minute. Pour off any excess fat.

2 Add the rice and fry, stirring briskly, for a further minute. Add the chicken stock and heat until boiling.

3 Thinly slice the chilli and trim the okra. Add to the pan with the tomato purée. Season to taste.

4 Return the chicken to the pan and stir. Cover tightly and simmer gently for 15 minutes, or until the rice is tender, the chicken is thoroughly cooked and all the liquid absorbed. Stir occasionally and if the mixture becomes too dry, add a little extra stock to moisten. Serve immediately.

3

2

3

cook's tip

The whole chilli makes the dish hot and spicy — if you prefer a milder flavour, discard the seeds.

variation

You can replace the chicken with 250 g/9 oz peeled prawns and 90 g/3 oz belly of pork, if desired. Slice the pork and fry in the oil before adding the onions, and add the prawns 5 minutes before the end of cooking time.

chilli coconut chicken

Coconut adds a creamy texture and delicious flavour to this Thai-style stir-fry, which is spiked with green chilli.

Serves 4

3 tbsp sesame oil

350 g/12 oz chicken breast, thinly sliced

salt and pepper

8 shallots, sliced

2 garlic cloves, finely chopped

2.5 cm/1 inch piece fresh root ginger, grated

1 green chilli, finely chopped

1 each red and green pepper, thinly sliced

3 courgettes, thinly sliced

2 tbsp ground almonds

1 tsp ground cinnamon

1 tbsp oyster sauce

50 g/1¾ oz creamed coconut, grated

1 Heat the sesame oil in a wok, add the chicken, season with salt and pepper, and stir-fry for about 4 minutes.

2 Add the shallots, garlic, ginger and chilli and stir-fry for 2 minutes.

3 Add the peppers and courgettes and cook for about 1 minute.

4 Finally, add the remaining ingredients and seasoning. Stir-fry for 1 minute and serve.

2

3

4

cook's tip

Creamed coconut is sold in blocks by supermarkets and oriental stores. It is a useful storecupboard standby as it adds richness and depth of flavour.

cook's tip

Since most of the heat of chillies comes from the seeds, remove them before cooking if you want a milder flavour. Be very careful when handling chillies — do not touch your face or eyes as the chilli juice can be very painful. Always wash your hands after preparing chillies.

fragrant chicken & broad beans

This is a quick and tasty way to use leftover roast chicken. The sauce can also be used for any cooked poultry, lamb or beef.

Serves 4

1 tsp mustard oil

3 tbsp vegetable oil

1 large onion, chopped finely

3 garlic cloves, crushed

1 tbsp tomato purée

2 tomatoes, peeled and chopped

1 tsp ground turmeric

½ tsp cumin seeds, ground

½ tsp coriander seeds, ground

½ tsp chilli powder

½ tsp garam masala

1 tsp red wine vinegar

1 small red pepper, chopped

125 g/4 oz frozen broad beans

500 g/1 lb cooked chicken breasts,
   cut into bite-sized pieces

salt

fresh coriander sprigs, to garnish

1 Heat the mustard oil in a large, frying pan set over a high heat for about 1 minute until it begins to smoke. Add the vegetable oil, reduce the heat and then add the onion and the garlic. Fry the garlic and onion until they are golden.

2 Add the tomato purée, chopped tomatoes, ground turmeric, cumin and coriander seeds, chilli powder, garam masala and red wine vinegar to the frying pan. Stir the mixture until fragrant.

3 Add the red pepper and broad beans and stir for 2 minutes until the pepper is softened. Stir in the chicken, and salt to taste. Leave to simmer gently for 6-8 minutes until the chicken is heated through and the beans are tender.

2

3

4 Serve garnished with coriander leaves.

cook's tip

This dish is an ideal way of making use of leftover poultry — turkey, duck or quail. Any variety of beans works well, but vegetables are just as useful, especially root vegetables, courgettes, potatoes or broccoli. Leafy vegetables will not be so successful.

1

sweet and sour chicken nuggets

Tender chicken nuggets are served with a sweet and sour sauce.

Serves 4

450 g/1 lb lean chicken, minced

   4 spring onions, trimmed and finely

   chopped

1 small red chilli, deseeded and finely

   chopped

2.5 cm/1 inch piece root ginger, finely

   chopped

salt and white pepper

100 g/3½ oz can sweetcorn (no added sugar

   or salt), drained

boiled jasmine rice and chives, snipped,

   to serve

SAUCE

150 ml/5 fl oz fresh chicken stock

100 g/3½ oz cubed pineapple in natural

   juice, drained, with 4 tbsp reserved juice

1 medium carrot, cut into thin strips

1 small red pepper, deseeded and diced

1 small green pepper, deseeded and diced

1 tbsp light soy sauce

2 tbsp rice vinegar

1 tbsp caster sugar

1 tbsp tomato purée

2 tsp cornflour mixed to a paste with 4 tsp

   cold water

2

1 To make the meatballs, place the chicken in a bowl and add the spring onions, chilli, ginger, seasoning and sweetcorn. Mix together with your hands.

2 Divide the mixture into 16 portions and form each into a ball. Bring a saucepan of water to the boil. Arrange the meatballs on a sheet of baking parchment in a steamer or large sieve, place over the water, cover and steam for 10–12 minutes.

3 To make the sauce, pour the stock and pineapple juice into a saucepan and bring to the boil. Add the carrot and peppers, cover and simmer for 5 minutes.

2

3

4 Stir in the remaining ingredients and heat through, stirring, until thickened. Season and set aside until required.

5 Drain the meatballs and transfer to a serving plate. Garnish with snipped chives and serve with boiled rice and the sauce (reheated if necessary).

japanese chicken & vegetables

This simple, Japanese style of cooking is ideal for thinly sliced breast of chicken. Mirin is a rich, sweet rice wine which is available from oriental shops.

Serves 4

4 boneless chicken breasts

1 red pepper

1 green pepper

4 spring onions

8 baby corn cobs

100 g/3½ oz beansprouts

1 tbsp sesame or sunflower oil

4 tbsp soy sauce

4 tbsp mirin

1 tbsp grated fresh ginger root

variation

If you cannot find mirin add one tablespoon of soft, light brown sugar to the sauce instead.

variation

Instead of serving the sauce as a dip, you could use it as a marinade. However, do not leave it to marinate for more than 2 hours as the soy sauce will cause the chicken to dry out and become tough. Use other vegetables, such as mangetout or thinly sliced carrots, if you prefer.

1

2

1 Remove the skin from the chicken and slice at a slight angle, to a thickness of about 5 mm/¼ inch.

2 Deseed and thinly slice the peppers and trim and slice the spring onions and sweetcorn. Arrange the peppers, spring onions, corn cobs and beansprouts on a plate with the sliced chicken.

3 Heat a large griddle or heavy frying pan then lightly brush with oil. Add the vegetables and chicken slices in small batches, allowing space between them so that they cook thoroughly.

4 In a small bowl, mix together the soy sauce, mirin and ginger and serve as a dip with the chicken and vegetables.

4

mexican chilli drumsticks

Chilli, tomatoes and corn are typical ingredients in a Mexican dish.

Serves 4

---

2 tbsp oil

8 chicken drumsticks

1 medium onion, finely chopped

1 tsp chilli powder

1 tsp ground coriander

400 g/14 oz can chopped tomatoes

2 tbsp tomato purée

125 g/4½ oz frozen sweetcorn

salt and pepper

rice and mixed pepper salad, to serve

---

cook's tip

Mexican dishes are not usually suitable for freezing because the strong flavours they contain, such as chilli, intensify during freezing, and if left for too long, an unpleasant, musty flavour can develop.

1

2

3

1 Heat the oil in a large frying pan, add the chicken drumsticks and cook over a medium heat until lightly browned. Remove the chicken drumsticks from the pan with a slotted spoon and set aside until required.

2 Add the chopped onion to the pan and cook for 3–4 minutes until softened, then stir in the chilli powder and coriander and cook for a few seconds, stirring briskly so the spices do not burn on the bottom of the pan. Add the chopped tomatoes with their juice and the tomato purée and stir well to incorporate.

3 Return the chicken drumsticks to the pan and simmer the casserole gently for 20 minutes until the chicken is tender and thoroughly cooked. Add the sweetcorn and cook for a further 3–4 minutes. Season with salt and pepper to taste.

4 Serve with rice and mixed pepper salad.

chow mein with chicken & shiitake mushrooms

No noodle section of an Oriental book would be complete without a Chow Mein recipe. This classic dish requires no introduction as it is already a favourite amongst most Chinese food-eaters.

Serves 4

250 g/9 oz packet of medium egg noodles

2 tbsp sunflower oil

275 g/9½ oz cooked chicken breasts,
   shredded

1 clove garlic, finely chopped

1 red pepper, deseeded and thinly sliced

100 g/3½ oz shiitake mushrooms, sliced

6 spring onions, sliced

100 g/3½ oz beansprouts

3 tbsp soy sauce

1 tbsp sesame oil

1

4

5

variation

You can make the chow mein
with a selection of vegetables
for a vegetarian dish, if you
prefer.

1 Place the egg noodles in a large
bowl or dish and break them up
slightly.

2 Pour enough boiling water over the
noodles to cover and leave to stand
whilst preparing the other ingredients.

3 Heat the sunflower oil in a large
preheated wok.

4 Add the shredded chicken, finely
chopped garlic, pepper slices,
mushrooms, spring onions and
beansprouts to the wok and stir-fry for
about 5 minutes.

5 Drain the noodles thoroughly. Add
the noodles to the wok, toss well
and stir-fry for a further 5 minutes.

6 Drizzle the soy sauce and sesame
oil over the chow mein and toss
until well combined.

7 Transfer the chicken chow mein to
warm serving bowls and serve
immediately.

chinese chicken in tangy lemon sauce

This is on everyone's list of favourite Chinese dishes, and it is so simple to make. Fried chicken is cooked in a tangy lemon sauce in minutes and is great served with stir-fried vegetables.

Serves 4

vegetable oil, for deep-frying

650 g/1½ lb skinless, boneless chicken,
    cut into strips

lemon slices and shredded spring onion,
    to garnish

SAUCE

1 tbsp cornflour

6 tbsp cold water

3 tbsp fresh lemon juice

2 tbsp sweet sherry

½ tsp caster sugar

cook's tip

If you would prefer to use
chicken portions rather than
strips, cook them in the oil,
covered, over a low heat for
about 30 minutes, or until
cooked through.

1 Heat the oil in a preheated wok until almost smoking. Reduce the heat and stir-fry the chicken strips for 3–4 minutes, until cooked through. Remove the chicken with a slotted spoon, set aside and keep warm. Drain the oil from the wok.

2 To make the sauce, mix the cornflour with 2 tablespoons of the water to form a paste.

3 Pour the lemon juice and remaining water into the mixture in the wok. Add the sherry and sugar and bring to the boil, stirring until the sugar has completely dissolved.

1

3

4

4 Stir in the cornflour mixture and return to the boil. Reduce the heat and simmer, stirring constantly, for 2-3 minutes, until the sauce is thickened and clear.

5 Transfer the chicken to a warm serving plate and pour the sauce over the top. Garnish with the lemon slices and shredded spring onion and serve immediately.

chicken & pineapple curry

Serve this fruity curry with mango chutney and naan bread, and top the curry with seedless grapes. Mangoes or pears make a good substitute for pineapple.

Serves 4-6

1 tbsp oil

900 g/2 lb chicken meat, chopped

60 g/2 oz/4 tbsp flour, seasoned

32 shallots, roughly chopped

4 garlic cloves, crushed with a little olive oil

3 cooking apples, diced

1 pineapple, diced

125 g/4½ oz sultanas

1 tbsp clear honey

300 ml/½ pint chicken stock

2 tbsp Worcestershire sauce

3 tbsp hot curry paste

salt and pepper

150 ml/¼ pint soured cream

rice, to serve

orange slices, to garnish

1 Heat the oil in a large frying pan. Coat the meat in the seasoned flour and cook for about 4 minutes until it is browned all over. Transfer the chicken to a large deep casserole and keep warm until required.

2 Slowly fry the shallots, garlic, apples, pineapple and sultanas in the pan juices.

3 Add the honey, chicken stock, Worcestershire sauce and hot curry paste. Season to taste with salt and pepper.

4 Pour the sauce over the chicken and cover the casserole with a lid or cooking foil.

5 Cook in the centre of a preheated oven, 180°C/350°F/Gas Mark 4, for about 2 hours. Stir in the soured cream and cook for a further 15 minutes. Serve the curry with rice, garnished with a slice of orange.

variation

Coconut rice also makes an excellent accompaniment to this dish. Place 25 g/1 oz chopped creamed coconut, 1 cinnamon stick, 600 ml/ 1 pint water in a large saucepan and bring to the boil. Stir in 350 g/12 oz basmati rice, cover and simmer gently for 15 minutes until all the liquid has been absorbed. Remove the cinnamon stick before serving.

2

3

5

indian roast chicken

This chicken dish, ideal for dinner parties, is cooked in the oven — which is very rare in Indian cooking. The chicken can be boned, if desired.

Serves 4

50 g/1¾ oz ground almonds

50 g/1¾ oz desiccated coconut

150 ml/¼ pint oil

1 medium onion, finely chopped

1 tsp fresh ginger root, chopped

1 tsp fresh garlic, crushed

1 tsp chilli powder

1½ tsp garam masala

1 tsp salt

150 ml/5 fl oz yogurt

4 chicken quarters, skinned

fresh coriander leaves and 1 lemon, cut into
    wedges, to garnish

green salad leaves, to serve

1 In a heavy-based saucepan, dry roast the ground almonds and coconut and set aside.

2 Heat the oil in a frying pan and fry the onion, stirring, until golden brown.

1

3

5

3 Place the ginger, garlic, chilli powder, garam masala and salt in a bowl and mix with the yogurt. Add the almonds and coconut and mix well.

4 Add the onions to the spice mixture, blend and set aside.

5 Arrange the chicken quarters in the bottom of a heatproof dish. Spoon the spice mixture over the chicken sparingly.

6 Cook in a pre-heated oven, 160°C/425°F/Gas Mark 3, for 35-45 minutes. Check that the chicken is cooked thoroughly by piercing the thickest part of the meat with a sharp knife or a fine skewer – the juices will run clear when the chicken is cooked through. Garnish with the coriander and lemon wedges and serve with a salad.

cook's tip

If you want a more spicy dish, add more chilli powder and garam masala.

india chicken & sultana pilaf

This is a simple version of a creamy textured and mildly spiced Indian pilau. Although there are lots of ingredients, there's very little preparation needed for this dish.

Serves 4

60 g/2 oz/4 tbsp butter

8 skinless, boneless chicken thighs, cut into
   large pieces

1 medium onion, sliced

1 tsp ground turmeric

1 tsp ground cinnamon

250 g/9 oz long grain rice

salt and pepper

425 ml/¾ pint natural yogurt

60 g/2 oz sultanas

200 ml/7 fl oz chicken stock

1 medium tomato, chopped

2 tbsp chopped fresh coriander or parsley

2 tbsp toasted coconut

fresh coriander, to garnish

1

2

3

1 Heat the butter in a heavy or non-stick pan and fry the chicken with the onion for about 3 minutes.

2 Stir in the turmeric, cinnamon, rice and seasoning and fry gently for 3 minutes.

3 Add the natural yogurt, sultanas and chicken stock and mix well. Cover and simmer for 10 minutes, stirring occasionally until the rice is tender and all the stock has been absorbed. Add more stock if the mixture becomes too dry.

4 Stir in the chopped tomato and fresh coriander or parsley.

5 Sprinkle the pilau with the toasted coconut and garnish with fresh coriander.

cook's tip

Long-grain rice is the most widely available and the cheapest rice. Basmati, with its slender grains and aromatic flavour, is more expensive and should be used on special occasions if it is not affordable on a frequent basis. Rice, especially basmati, should be washed thoroughly under cold, running water before use.

herbed chicken drumsticks with vegetables

One of my favourite dinner-party dishes, this is very attractive to look at. It should ideally be cooked and served from a karahi, but if you do not have one a deep, heavy frying-pan will do.

Serves 4

8 chicken drumsticks

1½ tsp fresh ginger root, finely chopped

1½ tsp fresh garlic, crushed

1 tsp salt

2 medium onions, chopped

½ large bunch fresh coriander leaves

4-6 green chillies

600 ml/1 pint oil

4 firm tomatoes, cut into wedges

2 large green peppers, roughly chopped

3 Heat the oil in a karahi or large frying pan. Add the remaining onions and fry until golden brown. Remove the onions from the pan with a perforated spoon and set aside.

4 Reduce the heat to medium hot and fry the chicken pieces, in batches of about 2 at a time, until cooked through (about 5–7 minutes per piece).

3

5 When all of the chicken pieces are cooked through, remove them from the pan, keep warm and set aside.

6 Add the tomatoes and the peppers to the pan and half-cook them until they are softened but still have 'bite'.

7 Transfer the tomatoes and peppers to a serving plate and arrange the chicken on top. Garnish with the reserved fried onions.

1 Make 2–3 slashes in each piece of chicken. Rub the ginger, garlic and salt over the chicken pieces and set aside.

2 Place half of the onions, the coriander leaves and green chillies in a pestle and mortar and grind to a paste. Rub the paste over the chicken pieces.

1

2

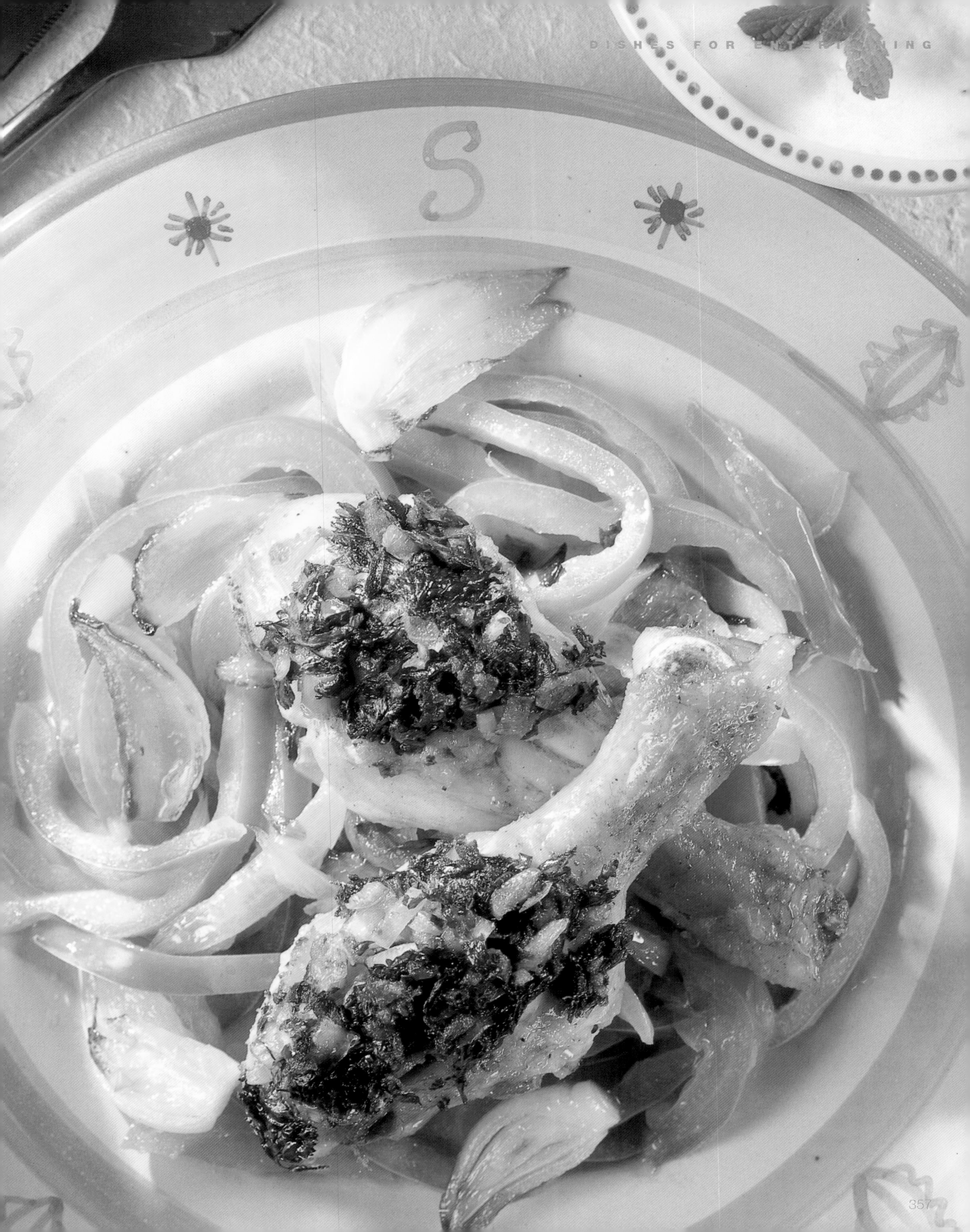

curried chicken korma with coriander

Korma is a typically mild and aromatic curry. If you want to reduce the fat in this recipe, use natural yogurt instead of the cream.

Serves 4-6

750 g/1 lb 10 oz chicken meat, cut
   into cubes

300 ml/½ pint double cream

½ tsp garam masala

KORMA PASTE

2 garlic cloves

2.5 cm/1 inch fresh ginger root,
   coarsely chopped

50 g/1¾ oz blanched almonds

6 tbsp chicken stock

1 tsp ground cardomon

4 cloves, crushed

1 tsp cinnamon

2 large onions, chopped

1 tsp coriander seeds

2 tsp ground cumin seeds

pinch cayenne

6 tbsp olive oil

salt and pepper

coriander, to garnish

rice, to serve

1 Place all the ingredients for the korma paste into a blender or food processor and blend together until a very smooth paste is formed.

2 Place the cubes of chicken in a bowl and pour over the korma paste. Stir to coat the chicken completely with the paste. Cover and chill in the refrigerator for 3 hours to allow the flavours to permeate the chicken.

1

2

4

3 Simmer the meat in a large saucepan for 25 minutes, adding a little chicken stock if the mixture becomes too dry.

4 Add the double cream and garam masala to the pan and simmer for a further 15 minutes. Allow the korma to stand for 10 minutes before serving. Garnish the chicken korma with fresh coriander and serve with rice.

cook's tip

Garam masala is the name given to the mixture of spices commonly used as a base in curries. It can be bought ready-mixed or you can prepare your own by grinding together 1 tsp cardamon seeds, 2 tsp cloves, 2 tbsp each cumin seeds and coriander seeds, 7.5 cm/3 inch piece cinnamon stick, 1 tbsp black peppercorns and 1 dried red chilli.

thai coconut chicken with lime & peanut sauce

This tasty Thai-style dish has a classic sauce of lime, peanut, coconut and chilli. You'll find coconut cream in most supermarkets or delicatessens.

Serves 4

150 ml/¼ pint hot chicken stock

30 g/1 oz coconut cream

1 tbsp sunflower oil

8 skinless, boneless chicken thighs,
    cut into long, thin strips

1 small red chilli, sliced thinly

4 spring onions, sliced thinly

4 tbsp smooth or crunchy peanut butter

finely grated rind and juice of 1 lime

boiled rice, to serve

spring onion flower and red chilli, to garnish

1 Place the chicken stock in a measuring jug and crumble the creamed coconut into the stock, stirring to dissolve.

2 Heat the oil in a wok or large heavy frying pan and cook the chicken strips, stirring, until golden.

3 Add the sliced red chilli and the spring onions to the pan and cook gently for a few minutes, stirring to mix all the ingredients.

4 Add the peanut butter, coconut cream, lime rind and juice and simmer uncovered, stirring, for about 5 minutes.

5 Serve with boiled rice, garnished with a spring onion flower and a red chilli.

3

4

1

variation

Limes are used frequently in Thai cookery, particularly in conjunction with sweet flavours such as coconut or peanut. They are used in preference to lemons because they have a more acidic flavour which lends freshness and tartness to many dishes. If limes are unavailable, you can use lemons instead.

spicy roast chicken with garlic & cashew nuts

Most of the flavourful stuffing is cooked separately from the chicken;
only a small amount is added to the neck end.

Serves 4

1 chicken, weighing about 1.5 kg/3 lb 5 oz

1 small onion, halved

25 g/1 oz butter, melted

1 tsp ground turmeric

1 tsp ground ginger

½ tsp cayenne

salt and pepper

fresh coriander, to garnish

STUFFING

2 tbsp oil

1 medium onion, chopped finely

½ medium red pepper, chopped finely

2 garlic cloves, crushed

125 g/4½ oz basmati rice

350 ml/12 fl oz hot chicken stock

grated rind of ½ lemon

½ tsp ground turmeric

½ tsp ground ginger

½ tsp ground coriander

pinch cayenne pepper

90 g/3 oz salted cashew nuts

2

2

3

1 To make the stuffing, heat the oil in
a saucepan, add the onion, red
pepper and garlic and cook gently for
4–5 minutes. Add the rice and stir to
coat in the oil. Add the stock, bring to
the boil, then simmer for 15 minutes
until all the liquid is absorbed. Transfer
to a bowl and add the remaining
ingredients for the stuffing. Season
well with pepper.

2 Place half the stuffing in the neck
end of the chicken and secure with
a cocktail stick. Put the halved onion
into the cavity of the chicken. Spoon the
rest of the rice stuffing into a greased
ovenproof dish and cover with foil.

3 Place the chicken in a roasting tin.
Prick all over avoiding the stuffed
area. Mix the butter and spices, season,
then brush over the chicken.

4 Roast in a preheated oven,
190°C/375°F/Gas Mark 5, for
1 hour, basting from time to time.
Place the dish of rice stuffing in the
oven and continue cooking the chicken
for 30 minutes. Remove the cocktail
stick and serve the chicken with stuffing
and gravy.

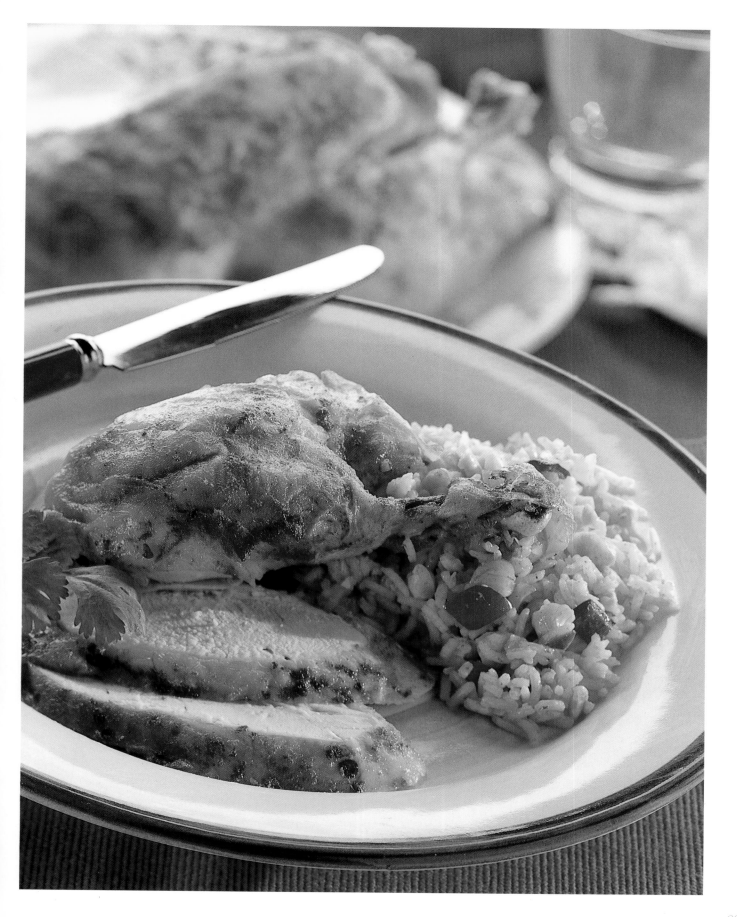

spicy grilled chicken tikka

For this very popular dish, small pieces of chicken are marinated for a minimum of 3 hours in yogurt and spices.

Serves 6

- 1 tsp fresh ginger root, finely chopped
- 1 tsp fresh garlic, crushed
- ½ tsp ground coriander
- ½ tsp ground cumin
- 1 tsp chilli powder
- 3 tbsp yogurt
- 1 tsp salt
- 2 tbsp lemon juice
- a few drops of red food colouring (optional)
- 1 tbsp tomato purée
- 1.5 kg/3 lb 5 oz chicken breast
- 1 onion, sliced
- 3 tbsp oil
- 6 lettuce leaves, to serve
- 1 lemon, cut into wedges, to garnish

cook's tip

Chicken tikka can be served with shop-bought naan breads and chutney and Raita (a mixture of chopped garlic and cucumber with natural yogurt).

2

3

1 Blend together the ginger, garlic, ground coriander, ground cumin and chilli powder in a large mixing bowl.

2 Add the yogurt, salt, lemon juice, red food colouring (if using) and the tomato purée to the spice mixture.

3 Using a sharp knife, cut the chicken into pieces. Add the chicken to the spice mixture and toss to coat well. Leave to marinate for at least 3 hours, preferably overnight.

4 Arrange the onion in the bottom of a heatproof dish. Carefully drizzle half of the oil over the onions.

5 Arrange the marinated chicken pieces on top of the onions and cook under a pre-heated grill, turning once and basting with the remaining oil, for 25-30 minutes.

3

6 Serve on a bed of lettuce and garnish with the lemon wedges.

chilli chicken with mushrooms & noodles

This tasty chicken stir-fry is quick and easy to make and is full of fresh flavours and crunchy vegetables.

Serves 4

400 g/14 oz chicken breasts, sliced thinly

pinch of salt

pinch of cornflour

2 tbsp oil

1 garlic clove, crushed

1 tbsp black bean sauce

1 each small red and green pepper,
    cut into strips

1 red chilli, chopped finely

75 g/2¾ oz mushrooms, sliced

1 onion, chopped

6 spring onions, chopped

fresh noodles, to serve

SEASONING

½ tsp salt

½ tsp sugar

3 tbsp chicken stock

1 tbsp dark soy sauce

2 tbsp beef stock

2 tbsp rice wine

1 tsp cornflour, blended with a little rice wine

1 Put the chicken strips in a bowl. Add a pinch of salt and a pinch of cornflour and cover with water. Leave for 30 minutes.

2 Heat 1 tbsp of the oil in a wok or deep-sided frying pan and stir-fry the chicken for 4 minutes. Transfer the chicken to a warm serving dish and clean the wok or pan.

3

1

2

3 Add the remaining oil to the wok and add the garlic, black bean sauce, green and red peppers, chilli, mushrooms, onion and spring onions. Stir-fry the vegetables for 2 minutes then return the chicken strips to the wok.

4 Add the seasoning, fry for 3 minutes and thicken with a little of the cornflour paste. Serve with fresh noodles.

cook's tip

Black bean sauce can be found in specialist shops and in many supermarkets. Use dried noodles if you can't find fresh noodles.

shredded chicken & red pepper with noodles

Blanched noodles are fried in the wok until crisp and brown, and then topped with a shredded chicken sauce for a delightfully tasty dish.

2

2

Serves 4

225 g/8 oz skinless, boneless chicken
    breasts, shredded

1 egg white

5 tsp cornflour

225 g/8 oz thin egg noodles

320 ml/11 fl oz vegetable oil

600 ml/1 pint chicken stock

2 tbsp dry sherry

2 tbsp oyster sauce

1 tbsp light soy sauce

1 tbsp hoisin sauce

1 red pepper, seeded and very thinly sliced

2 tbsp water

3 spring onions, chopped

1 Mix the chicken, egg white and
2 teaspoons of the cornflour in a
bowl. Let stand for at least 30 minutes.

2 Blanch the noodles in boiling water
for 2 minutes, then drain thoroughly.
Heat 300 ml/½ pint of the oil in a
preheated wok. Add the noodles,
spreading them to cover the base of
the wok. Cook over a low heat for
about 5 minutes, until the noodles are
browned on the underside. Flip the
noodles over and brown on the other
side. Remove from the wok when
crisp and browned, place on a serving
plate and keep warm. Drain the oil from
the wok.

3 Add 300 ml/½ pint of the chicken
stock to the wok. Remove from the
heat and add the chicken, stirring well
so that it does not stick. Return to the
heat and cook for 2 minutes. Drain,
discarding the stock.

4 Wipe the wok with kitchen paper
and return to the heat. Add the
sherry, oyster sauce, soy sauce, hoisin
sauce, red pepper and the remaining
chicken stock and bring to the boil.
Blend the remaining cornflour with the
water to form a paste and stir it into
the mixture.

5 Return the chicken to the wok and
cook over a low heat for 2 minutes.
Place the chicken on top of the noodles
and sprinkle with spring onions. Serve
immediately.

5

chicken, sage & mushroom pie

This pie has an attractive filo pastry case which has a 'ruffled' top made with strips of the pastry brushed with melted butter.

Serves 4

---

225 g/8 oz waxy potatoes, cubed

60 g/2 oz butter

1 skinned chicken breast fillet, about
    175 g/6 oz, cubed

1 leek, sliced

150 g/5½ oz chestnut mushrooms, sliced

25 g/1 oz plain flour

300 ml/½ pint milk

1 tbsp Dijon mustard

2 tbsp chopped fresh sage

225 g/8 oz filo pastry, thawed if frozen

40 g/1½ oz butter, melted

salt and pepper

---

cook's tip

If the top of the pie starts
to brown too quickly, cover it
with foil halfway through the
cooking time, to allow the
pastry base to cook through
without the top burning.

1 Cook the potato cubes in a saucepan of boiling water for 5 minutes. Drain and set aside.

2 Melt the butter in a frying pan and cook the chicken cubes for 5 minutes or until browned all over.

3 Add the leek and mushrooms and cook for 3 minutes, stirring. Stir in the flour and cook for 1 minute. Gradually add the milk and bring to the boil. Add the mustard, chopped sage and potato cubes, then leave the mixture to simmer for 10 minutes.

3

4

5

4 Meanwhile, line a deep pie dish with half of the sheets of filo pastry. Spoon the sauce into the dish and cover with one sheet of pastry. Brush the pastry with butter and lay another sheet on top. Brush this sheet with butter.

5 Cut the remaining filo pastry into strips and fold them on to the top of the pie to create a ruffled effect. Brush the strips with the melted butter and cook in a preheated oven 180°C/350°F/ Gas Mark 4 for 45 minutes or until golden brown and crisp. Serve hot.

chicken & water chestnuts in ginger liquor

This is a spicy casserole of rice, chicken, vegetables and chilli in a soy and ginger flavoured liquor. Although called a casserole, the dish only requires approximately 30 minutes cooking time.

Serves 4

150 g/5½ oz long-grain rice

1 tbsp dry sherry

2 tbsp light soy sauce

2 tbsp dark soy sauce

2 tsp dark brown sugar

1 tsp salt

1 tsp sesame oil

900 g/2 lb skinless, boneless chicken meat, diced

850 ml/1½ pints chicken stock

2 open-cap mushrooms, sliced

60 g/2 oz water chestnuts, halved

75 g/3 oz broccoli florets

1 yellow pepper, sliced

4 tsp grated fresh root ginger

whole chives, to garnish

1 Cook the rice in a saucepan of boiling water for about 15 minutes. Drain well, rinse under cold water and drain again thoroughly.

2 Place the sherry, soy sauces, sugar, salt and sesame oil in a large bowl and mix together until well combined.

3 Stir the chicken into the soy mixture, turning to coat well. Leave to marinate for about 30 minutes.

4 Bring the stock to the boil in a saucepan or preheated wok.

5 Add the chicken with the marinade, mushrooms, water chestnuts, broccoli, pepper and ginger.

3

6

6 Stir in the rice, reduce the heat, cover and cook for 25–30 minutes, until the chicken and vegetables are cooked through.

7 Transfer to serving plates, garnish with chives and serve.

variation

This dish would work equally well with beef or pork. Chinese dried mushrooms may be used instead of the open-cap mushrooms, if rehydrated before adding to the dish.

2

mashed potato & chicken cakes

Potato cakes are a great favourite, but are usually served plain as a side dish. In this recipe the potatoes are combined with minced chicken and mashed banana for a fruit-flavoured main course.

Serves 4

450 g/1 lb floury potatoes, diced

225 g/8 oz minced chicken

1 large banana

2 tbsp plain flour

1 tsp lemon juice

1 onion, finely chopped

2 tbsp chopped fresh sage

salt and pepper

25 g/1 oz/2 tbsp butter

2 tbsp vegetable oil

150 ml/¼ pint single cream

150 ml/¼ pint chicken stock

fresh sage leaves, to garnish

2

3

4

1 Cook the diced potatoes in a saucepan of boiling water for 10 minutes until cooked through. Drain and mash the potatoes until smooth. Stir in the chicken.

2 Mash the banana and add it to the potato with the flour, lemon juice, onion and half of the chopped sage. Season well and stir the mixture together.

3 Divide the mixture into 8 equal portions. With lightly floured hands, shape each portion into a round patty.

4 Heat the butter and oil in a frying pan, add the potato cakes and cook for 12–15 minutes or until cooked through, turning once. Remove from the pan and keep warm.

5 Stir the cream and stock into the pan with the remaining chopped sage. Cook over a low heat for 2–3 minutes.

6 Arrange the potato cakes on a serving plate, garnish with fresh sage leaves and serve with the cream and sage sauce.

cook's tip

Do not boil the sauce once the cream has been added as it will curdle. Cook it gently over a very low heat.

chinese five-spice chicken

In this recipe, the chicken is brushed with a syrup and deep-fried until golden. It is a little time-consuming, but well worth the effort.

Serves 4

1.5 kg/3 lb 5 oz oven-ready chicken

2 tbsp clear honey

2 tsp Chinese five-spice powder

2 tbsp rice wine vinegar

850 ml/1½ pints vegetable oil, for frying

chilli sauce, to serve

cook's tip

If it is easier, use chicken portions instead of a whole chicken. You could also use chicken legs for this recipe, if you prefer.

1 Rinse the chicken inside and out under cold running water and pat dry with kitchen paper.

2 Bring a large saucepan of water to the boil and remove from the heat. Place the chicken in the water, cover and set aside for 20 minutes. Remove the chicken from the water and pat dry with kitchen paper. Cool and leave to chill in the refrigerator overnight.

3 To make the glaze, mix the honey, Chinese five-spice powder and rice wine vinegar.

4 Brush some of the glaze all over the chicken and return to the refrigerator for 20 minutes. Repeat this process until all of the glaze has been used up. Return the chicken to the refrigerator for at least 2 hours after the final coating.

2

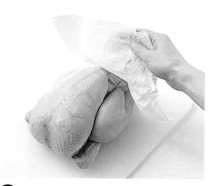

2

5

5 Using a cleaver or heavy kitchen knife, open the chicken out by splitting it through the centre through the breast and then cut each half into 4 pieces.

6 Heat the oil for deep-frying in a wok until almost smoking. Reduce the heat and fry each piece of chicken for 5–7 minutes, until golden and cooked through. Remove from the oil with a slotted spoon and drain on absorbent kitchen paper.

7 Transfer to a serving dish and serve hot with a little chilli sauce.

garlic & soy glazed chicken

This is a delicious way to cook a whole chicken. It has a wonderful glaze, which is served as a sauce.

Serves 4

1.5 kg/3 lb 5 oz chicken

3 tbsp vegetable oil

1 tbsp peanut oil

2 tbsp dark brown sugar

5 tbsp dark soy sauce

150 ml/¼ pint water

2 garlic cloves, crushed

1 small onion, chopped

1 fresh red chilli, chopped

celery leaves and chives, to garnish

2

3

2

cook's tip

When caramelising the sugar, do not turn the heat too high, otherwise it may burn.

1 Clean the chicken inside and out with damp kitchen paper.

2 Put the oils in a large wok, add the sugar and heat gently until the sugar caramelises. Stir in the soy sauce. Add the chicken and turn it in the mixture to coat thoroughly on all sides.

3 Add the water, garlic, onion and chilli. Cover and simmer, turning the chicken occasionally, for about 1 hour, or until cooked through. Test by piercing a thigh with the point of a knife or a skewer – the juices will run clear when the chicken is cooked.

4 Remove the chicken from the wok and set aside. Increase the heat and reduce the sauce in the wok until thickened. Transfer the chicken to a serving plate, garnish with celery leaves and chives and serve with the sauce.

variation

For a spicier sauce, add 1 tbsp finely chopped fresh root ginger and 1 tbsp ground Szechuan peppercorns with the chilli in step 3. If the flavour of dark soy sauce is too strong for your taste, substitute 2 tbsp dark soy sauce and 3 tbsp light soy sauce. This will result in a more delicate taste without sacrificing the attractive colour of the dish.

chicken, potato & white wine casserole

Small new potatoes are ideal for this recipe as they can be cooked whole.
If larger potatoes are used, cut them in half or into chunks before adding them
to the casserole.

Serves 4

2 tbsp vegetable oil

60 g/2 oz butter

4 chicken portions, about 225 g/8 oz each

2 leeks, sliced

1 garlic clove, crushed

4 tbsp plain flour

900 ml/1½ pints chicken stock

300 ml/½ pint dry white wine

125 g/4½ oz baby carrots, halved
   lengthways

125 g/4½ oz baby sweetcorn cobs,
   halved lengthways

450 g/1 lb small new potatoes

1 bouquet garni

150 ml/¼ pint double cream

salt and pepper

plain rice and fresh vegetables, to serve

cook's tip

Use turkey fillets instead of
the chicken, if preferred, and
vary the vegetables according
to those you have to hand.

1

3

5

1 Heat the oil and butter in a large
frying pan. Cook the chicken for
10 minutes, turning until browned all
over. Transfer the chicken to a casserole
dish using a perforated spoon.

2 Add the leek and garlic to the frying
pan and cook for 2–3 minutes,
stirring. Stir in the flour and cook for a
further 1 minute. Remove the frying pan
from the heat and stir in the stock and
wine. Season well.

3 Return the pan to the heat and
bring the mixture to the boil. Stir
in the carrots, sweetcorn, potatoes
and bouquet garni.

4 Transfer the mixture to the
casserole dish. Cover and cook
in a preheated oven, 180°C/350°F/
Gas Mark 4, for about 1 hour.

5 Remove the casserole from the
oven and stir in the cream. Return
the casserole to the oven, uncovered,
and cook for a further 15 minutes.
Remove the bouquet garni and discard.
Taste and adjust the seasoning, if
necessary. Serve the casserole with
plain rice or fresh vegetables, such
as broccoli.

chinese chicken with onion rice

This dish has a wonderful colour obtained from the turmeric, and a great spicy flavour, making it very appealing all round.

Serves 4

1 tbsp Chinese five-spice powder

2 tbsp cornflour

350 g/12 oz boneless, skinless chicken
  breasts, cubed

3 tbsp groundnut oil

1 onion, diced

225 g/8 oz long-grain white rice

½ tsp tumeric

600 ml/1 pint chicken stock

2 tbsp snipped fresh chives

cook's tip

Be careful when using turmeric
as it can stain the hands and
clothes a distinctive shade of
yellow.

1

2

5

1 Place the Chinese five-spice powder and cornflour in a large bowl. Add the chicken pieces and toss to coat all over.

2 Heat 2 tablespoons of the groundnut oil in a large preheated wok. Add the chicken pieces to the wok and stir-fry for 5 minutes. Using a slotted spoon, remove the chicken and set aside.

3 Add the remaining groundnut oil to the wok.

4 Add the onion to the wok and stir-fry for 1 minute.

5 Add the rice, tumeric and chicken stock to the wok and bring to the boil.

6 Return the chicken pieces to the wok, reduce the heat and leave to simmer for 10 minutes, or until the liquid has been absorbed and the rice is tender.

7 Add the chives, stir to mix and serve hot.

index